HERE'S TO
YOUR HEALTH

Margo Drummond

Galena Publishing
Galena, Illinois

ISBN: 0-9767954-4-2

Cover Photo: The "Milkmaid" image has been reproduced with the permission of GlaxoSmithKline. HORLICKS is a trademark of the Glaxo-SmithKline group of companies.

Photos on Back Cover: Courtesy of Sir John Horlick, England

Cover Design: Corey Bolle, Judy Moungey and Nancy Hoff

Galena Publishing
P. O. Box 18
Galena, IL 61036

Printed in the United States of America

This book is dedicated to the memory of
James and William Horlick.

Table of Contents

Acknowledgement

I would like to thank the following individuals, groups and organizations for their contributions to this endeavor. Though some may not be individually recognized, each of your names, nonetheless, belongs on this book. So it is with gratitude to and appreciation for:

Horlick family members Giles Weaver and Sir John Horlick.

English local historians Averil Kear and Andrew Gardiner.

Horlick's (Slough) curator, Karen Flintoff, Mohammed Saleem of Research and Development, and Paul Doneghan who kindly granted access to the facility.

Those who provided background information—the Racine Heritage Museum, the Racine Public Library, the University of Wisconsin-Parkside Archives, the State of Wisconsin Historical Society Archives, and the Offices of Mound and Graceland Cemeteries in Racine.

My publisher Sandra Principe who guided me through the process.

All who contributed stories, anecdotes, and access to items from their collections of Horlick memorabilia.

The outstanding language skills and expertise of editors Connie Eberly and Mary Neu.

An individual without whom the project could not have been completed, Judy Moungey—her dedication to seeing that every aspect of creating a perfect manuscript was accomplished in a timely and professional way was matched only by the energy and enthusiasm with which she went about it.

And most especially to my husband Jim who provided advice and encouragement along with the most generous gift of all, that of time, to insure that this was written.

Preface

"Here's to your health," William Horlick was known to say, as he showered friends and strangers alike with malted milk tablets drawn from his pocket. And so it was that just as John D. Rockefeller's habit of handing out shiny new coins made his name synonymous with wealth, the Horlick name on malted milk products became equated with health. For infants, invalids, astronauts, explorers, school children, soda fountain aficionados, and soldiers, as well as inhabitants of third world countries struggling to survive, there was a shared belief that good and safe nutrition and Horlick's were actually one in the same.

When he died at the age of 90, the *Miami Daily News* likened William Horlick's life to that of "an Horatio Alger" hero and his absolute faith in his product as "the reflection of almost a story-book quality." The same could easily have been said of his brother, James, who, together with William, built a business that produced one of the world's first processed foods. The world that they had known as children growing up in the tiny village of Ruardean would give way to a world of riches and royalty, of luxury and leisure, a world which, as the 19th century gave way to the 20th, would offer them experiences and opportunities beyond all imagining.

Today as we enter the 21st century, the name Horlick no longer holds claim to what it once did. Retro publications offer Horlick tablets for sale, Horlick items trade on e-Bay, and in their native England. Horlick's is still manufactured as part of the pharmaceutical giant, GlaxoSmithKline. The "technologically hip" generation, meanwhile, has likely never even heard of Horlick's other than perhaps in Great Britain. Things change, life moves on, and contemporary norms become relegated to the realm of nostalgia. Along the way, certain elements are lost.

The purpose of this writing is to record a story worth telling before it too is lost. In some sense it already is, for as one Horlick descendant observed, "You waited 80 years too long for this," a point well taken.

But absent of what might have been, there remains a vivid and fascinating tale of how two brothers, James and William Horlick, created for themselves and their families a future fashioned on inspiration, industry, fortitude and faith, all the while never forgetting their past and its profound influence upon them.

SIR JAMES HORLICK,

courtesy Giles Weaver (great-grandson of Sir James Horlick)

Sir James Horlick—from Vanity Fair Magazine
courtesy Giles Weaver (great-grandson of Sir James Horlick)

Margo Drummond

William Horlick
courtesy Racine Heritage Museum

4

William Horlick at Home in Racine
courtesy Racine Heritage Museum

Margo Drummond

Introduction—STREETS PAVED WITH GOLD

America during the Roaring 20's—a golden era of optimism, of jazz-crazed flappers with slim hips and gin flasks, commerce conducted over cocktails at the Cotton Club, college kids attending football games in fur coats and fedoras, shoot-outs and speakeasies and speculation—limousines, the Lindy and lavish excesses—global aviation and exploration, women's liberation and free-flowing libations indulged in by nearly all. The rich got richer. They spent millions on mansions, sailed in luxury liners across the seas, indulged their curiosities with travel to exotic places for extended periods of time, meanwhile investing and profiting beyond measure.

From the wealth generated during the early 1900's there emerged a large and growing middle class. Hard-working immigrant stock supplied the labor force necessary to keep America's industries humming. Savings provided for purchase of a home, a car, and perhaps even college educations for the kids. "Rich as Rockefeller" they might not be, but their opportunity to own a part of the so-called American dream would not be denied them.

Racine, Wisconsin, during the 1920's—beautifully situated on the shores of Lake Michigan between Chicago and Milwaukee—the typical American city peopled by natives of almost every country on earth, a community that came to be acclaimed as the "Belle City of the Lakes." Blessed with gifts from the glacial period some 10,000 years before, Racine, which means "root" in both the language of its early Native American inhabitants and that of the French explorers who followed them, was a truly solid and beautiful city as the second decade of the 20th century began. Artesian wells supplied essential fresh water; clay, lime, and stone could be readily quarried for building; an abundant supply of sand was available for industrial steel castings; rich agricultural soil produced wheat, corn, and barley along with fodder for dairy cows. Railways and waterways guaranteed easy access to the rest of the country. A seemingly endless flow of immigrant labor—Danes, Welsh, Germans, Irish, Bohemians, Italians (some 25 nationalities in all) rounded out the picture, their skills providing what 100 of the city's family-owned industries needed to move forward an already flourishing local economy. In the year 1911, Racine County was listed as one of the richest in the world, boasting a per capita holding of $790, with $36,000,000 in real estate.

Like so many of those laborers he would later employ, William Horlick came to America seeking his fortune amidst the proverbial streets paved with gold. And while some accounts say that young Horlick made the journey on his own, most seem to indicate that he was accompanied by an uncle, Joseph Alexander Horlick, who operated a lime and stone business along the Root River Rapids just north of Racine, known as Horlick's Lime and Stone.

Horlick's Lime and Stone—near the Root River Rapids, Racine, Wisconsin
courtesy Racine Heritage Museum

Joseph Alexander Horlick had emigrated to Racine from his native Gloucestershire, England in the early 1800's. Having successfully established a business, he reportedly made regular visits back to a place in Gloucestershire known as the Ross. On the 20th of July 1889 Joseph Alexander Horlick, aged 76, died at Wotton, near Gloucester.

Interestingly, the will of Joseph Alexander Horlick, written on August 16, 1870, while he was living in Racine County, did not mention a daughter, Arabella Roselia Horlick, as an inheritor, though it did include his wife, Arabella Roselia (Lediard) Horlick and sons, Joseph A., George, and Oliver J., along with another daughter, Emma. That will of Joseph Alexander Horlick was written exactly three months before the wedding of Arabella Roselia Horlick to her second cousin, William. Shortly after the ceremony, which was held in Mt. Pleasant, just outside Racine, William, then 23, and his bride, 21, sailed for England where they would remain until 1872. Or would they?

A possible explanation for the couple's return to America in 1871, if indeed they did return, was the Great Chicago Fire which occurred that year. Following the fire, a high demand for lime and stone arose, both needed to rebuild the ravaged city. Joseph Alexander Horlick may have sent his son-in-law William to oversee operations of the lime and stone company he had established in Chicago to meet those high demands.

In one account of William and Arabella's early life together, they were living in Chicago when the Great Fire occurred on October 9, 1871, and that, while most structures around them were destroyed, their house suffered damages limited to blistered paint. And yet, their first child, Alice Priscilla, was baptized on October 8, 1871, at Ruardean, England with her parents being listed as residents of Ross. Were William and Arabella in Chicago continuing work on a baby food formula that would bring them fortune and fame or was William, as records in Gloucestershire reflect, working as a saddle maker in England?

Whatever the case, forty years later as the Roaring 20's got underway, William Horlick, co-founder of the Horlick's Malted Milk Company, was living the dream that had lured so many, including him, to leave their homes for America. His Racine residence with its manicured gardens bordered the factory he had fashioned to resemble an English castle. Winters were spent at his Collins Avenue mansion in Miami. Luxurious trans-Atlantic voyages to his native England were frequent. Horlick's success and notoriety, however, paled by comparison to that of his only surviving daughter, Mabelle, who would make international

9

headlines over a lifestyle epitomizing the opulence and the excesses of the times in which she and her father lived.

Meanwhile, "across the pond," in England, William's older brother James and his family led equally sumptuous lives. James and William together had established the company bearing their name, a name synonymous with sustaining the health of infants, invalids, explorers, Olympic athletes, and World War I infantrymen—a product served up in soda fountain concoctions—a product known and trusted in Third World countries across the globe. The Horlick story, variously referred to as a romantic, rags-to-riches, Rockefeller style saga, is worth telling. To do so, let's begin where James and William Horlick did, in a tiny English village called Ruardean.

A Branch of the Horlick Family Tree

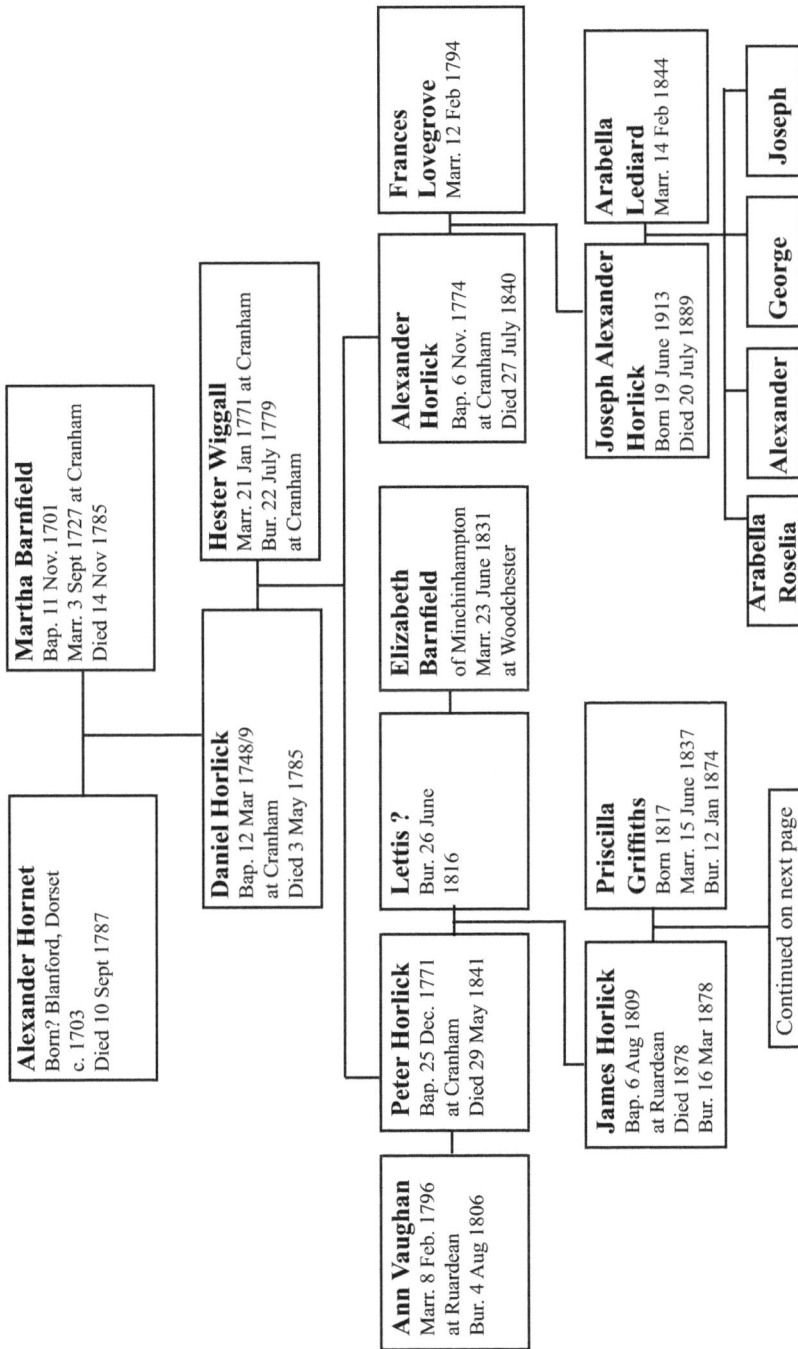

Alexander Hornet
Born? Blanford, Dorset
c. 1703
Died 10 Sept 1787

Martha Barnfield
Bap. 11 Nov. 1701
Marr. 3 Sept 1727 at Cranham
Died 14 Nov 1785

Daniel Horlick
Bap. 12 Mar 1748/9
at Cranham
Died 3 May 1785

Hester Wiggall
Marr. 21 Jan 1771 at Cranham
Bur. 22 July 1779
at Cranham

Peter Horlick
Bap. 25 Dec. 1771
at Cranham
Died 29 May 1841

Lettis ?
Bur. 26 June
1816

Ann Vaughan
Marr. 8 Feb. 1796
at Ruardean
Bur. 4 Aug 1806

James Horlick
Bap. 6 Aug 1809
at Ruardean
Died 1878
Bur. 16 Mar 1878

Priscilla Griffiths
Born 1817
Marr. 15 June 1837
Bur. 12 Jan 1874

Elizabeth Barnfield
of Minchinhampton
Marr. 23 June 1831
at Woodchester

Alexander Horlick
Bap. 6 Nov. 1774
at Cranham
Died 27 July 1840

Frances Lovegrove
Marr. 12 Feb 1794

Joseph Alexander Horlick
Born 19 June 1913
Died 20 July 1889

Arabella Lediard
Marr. 14 Feb 1844

Arabella Roselia

Alexander

George

Joseph

Continued on next page

11

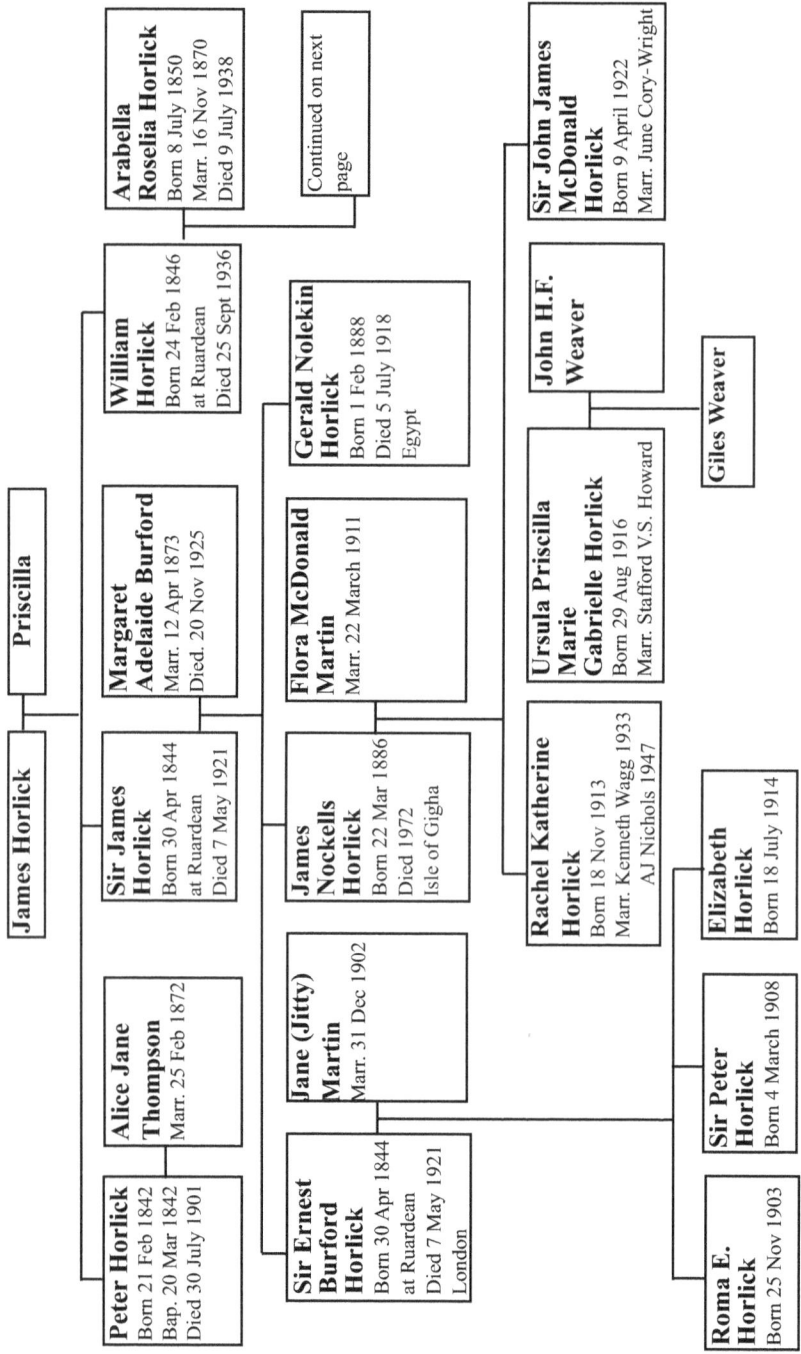

Priscilla

James Horlick

Arabella Roselia Horlick
Born 8 July 1850
Marr. 16 Nov 1870
Died 9 July 1938

Continued on next page

Sir John James McDonald Horlick
Born 9 April 1922
Marr. June Cory-Wright

William Horlick
Born 24 Feb 1846
at Ruardean
Died 25 Sept 1936

Gerald Nolekin Horlick
Born 1 Feb 1888
Died 5 July 1918
Egypt

John H.F. Weaver

Giles Weaver

Margaret Adelaide Burford
Marr. 12 Apr 1873
Died. 20 Nov 1925

Flora McDonald Martin
Marr. 22 March 1911

Ursula Priscilla Marie Gabrielle Horlick
Born 29 Aug 1916
Marr. Stafford V.S. Howard

Sir James Horlick
Born 30 Apr 1844
at Ruardean
Died 7 May 1921

James Nockells Horlick
Born 22 Mar 1886
Died 1972
Isle of Gigha

Rachel Katherine Horlick
Born 18 Nov 1913
Marr. Kenneth Wagg 1933
AJ Nichols 1947

Elizabeth Horlick
Born 18 July 1914

Alice Jane Thompson
Marr. 25 Feb 1872

Jane (Jitty) Martin
Marr. 31 Dec 1902

Peter Horlick
Born 21 Feb 1842
Bap. 20 Mar 1842
Died 30 July 1901

Sir Ernest Burford Horlick
Born 30 Apr 1844
at Ruardean
Died 7 May 1921
London

Sir Peter Horlick
Born 4 March 1908

Roma E. Horlick
Born 25 Nov 1903

12

James Horlick — Priscilla

Peter Horlick
Born 21 Feb 1842
Bap. 20 Mar 1842
Died 30 July 1901

Alice Jane
Thompson
Marr. 25 Feb 1872

William
Horlick
Born 24 Feb 1846
at Ruardean
Died 25 Sept 1936

Arabella
Roselia Horlick
Born 8 July 1850
Marr. 16 Nov 1870
Died 9 July 1938

Sir James
Horlick
Born 30 Apr 1844
at Ruardean
Died 7 May 1921

Margaret
Adelaide Burford
Marr. 12 Apr 1873
Died. 20 Nov 1925

Continued on
previous page

Alice Priscilla
Horlick
Born 8 Aug 1871
Died 10 Feb 1882

Alexander J.
(AJ) Horlick
Born 3 Oct 1873
Died 6 June 1950

Bertha
Hueffner
Born 10 Jan 1874
Marr. 16 Feb 1898
Died 20 Sep 1949

William
Horlick Jr.
Born 12 Dec 1875
Chicago, Illinois
Died 1 Apr 1940

Mabelle
Horlick
Born 15 April 1877
Died 6 July 1938

John Streeter
Sidley
Marr. 30 Jun 1909

William
Horlick Sidley
Born 31 Dec 1912
Died 13 Aug 1963

June
Anderson
Marr. 1942
Yuma, Arizona

Maureen Horlick
Sidley

Jeanette Horlick
Simmons
Born 9 May 1901
Racine

Zalmon
Guilbert
Simmons

Helen Bond
Born 16 Dec 1898
Racine

Harold
Sherman Bond
Marr. 26 Apr 1924
Chicago

James Horlick Bond

Patricia Simmons

Jeanette Simmons

Family Tree Designed by Andrew Kueffler

13

Margo Drummond

I. THE FOREST OF DEAN

When you stand outside the Horlick houses and the granary in Ruardean (which means "rural farmland"), it is possible on a clear day to see across to Wales. According to a history taken from Burke's Peerage:

> *the family name of Harlech or Horlick is of Norman-French derivation and the national conclusion drawn is that the Harlechs or Horlicks were primarily inhabitants of Normandy, and on leaving their own country settled in the country of Merionethshire, Wales, on whose coast the castle of Harlech now stands, partly in ruins. And in the long wars that followed the subjugation of Wales, the Harlechs were compelled to leave and settle in England which they did in Gloucestershire, where members of the Horlick family have long resided. (N 3 The Rocks Southwood), also Painswick, three miles from the ancient city of Gloucester, which is known by the numerous tombstones bearing the said name Cranham, three miles from Paiswick, same county, Ruardean, etc.*

The name of Harlech was immortalized in the song, "The March of the Men of Harlech" during the long feudal wars that followed the subjugation of Wales.

Members of the Horlick family first settled in Painswick sometime around 1680. Weavers by trade, their name was variously spelled as Hornet, Horneck and later Horlick. (See family tree on pages 11-13.) Alexander Hornet, who was born sometime around 1703, is believed to have been the one from whom most other Horlick family members in Gloucestershire were descended.

On September 3, 1727, at Cranham, Alexander Hornet married Martha Barnfield. Their son, Daniel Horlick, was the father of Peter Horlick. Peter's grandsons, James and William, would go on to create

15

the vast empire based on Horlick's malted milk products.

The homes of William and James Horlick's grandfather, Peter, and that of their father, James, stand side by side in Ruardean, across from the granary. That structure, half of which is known as Horlick House, dates back to 1777. Its high point in the village provides a view from the upstairs back windows of the coal mine known as True Blue. As well as being the oldest coal mining town in England, Ruardean was a major malting area. Malsters made beer and cider and a milky drink called grog, which was non-alcoholic. The malt needed for the process was secured by placing barley on damp stone floors causing it to sprout. From the sprouts the malters made malt.

The Horlick House—Ruardean, England
taken by the author

Peter Horlick came to Ruardean from the other side of Painswick (Cotswolds) sometime before 1796. He had been baptized in Cranham on December 25, 1771, and was likely the first member of the Horlick family to settle in Ruardean, though why is unknown. One theory is that the move resulted from his protest against the established church. According to an article printed in England in November of 2003:

The Granary—Ruardean, England
taken by the author

John Horlick, probably a removed cousin or great-uncle to William and James, was a leading religious dissenter, a Ranter. For some time he was innkeeper of the Angel and Colliers pubs, and oversaw the building of Ruardean's first non-conformist chapel (now closed and in disrepair) and was minister of Ruardean and Mitcheldean for at least 50 years after 1801. He was an unpublished chronicler and historian, and may well have been involved in riotous stone-throwing protests at establishment churches. The dissenters' stunts included organizing an impromptu country dance to drown out services at the church in Blakeney. It was said after John Horlick's death in 1858 that anyone who spoke ill of chapel folk would incur the wrath of his ghost.

On February 8, 1796, Peter Horlick married Ann Vaughn, the Vaughns being associated with the Childers Dynasty dating back to Henry V. The couple had four daughters before Ann's death at the age of 32 in 1806. Following Ann's death, Peter married Lettis (Lettice, sp.) Vaughn (possibly Ann's sister). Lettis' maiden name remains in question as the wedding took place outside the county, but local Ruardean historians think that her name was indeed Vaughn. Whatever the case may be, Lettis and Peter Horlick became parents of a son whom they named James, baptized on August 6, 1809, at Ruardean. Lettis Horlick died in 1816 at the age of 44, leaving Peter a widower once again. On June 23, 1831, at Woodchester, Peter Horlick married for a third time. His bride, Elizabeth Barnfield of Minchinhampton, was likely connected in some way to the Martha Barnfield who had married Peter's grandfather, Alexander Hornet, some 104 years before.

The Horlicks of Ruardean were so-called movers and shakers. Peter Horlick "had his fingers in some lucrative pies including farming, brewing and local government... The 1831 census for Ruardean shows that from just 127 families, 160 people were on poor relief. But the land-owning Horlick family practically controlled Ruardean—playing pivotal roles in chapel, court, brewery and agriculture."

Peter Horlick's own grandsons, James and William, were two of nine children born to James and Priscilla (Griffiths) Horlick. Both Priscilla and James had grown up in Ruardean where James would later make his living as a harness and saddle maker, a skill he passed on to his son William. Like other residents of the area, the Horlicks had pear and apple orchards. Grandfather Peter taught his grandsons, William, James, and Peter, the process of malting necessary to make apple and pear cider as well as beer. The old man's knowledge of the malting process likely came from a family background in baking that required the use of yeast.

Bucolic best describes the area of Ruardean where the sons of James and Priscilla Horlick spent their childhoods. Surrounded by rolling hills and ancient forests were the apple and pear orchards that still contain old stone presses used to extract the juice of the fruit. A pub claiming to be the oldest in England likewise remains. Begun in the year 1111, it is appropriately named the "Malt Shovel."

West End Ruardean
courtesy Racine Heritage Museum

The 12th century Norman cathedral of Ruardean, St. John the Baptist, is still actively worshipped in. Its eight bells are rung by hand, two of them having been donated by James and William Horlick in 1905. Alongside the church lies a graveyard where Peter Horlick as well as his three wives are buried. Nearby are the graves of James and Priscilla Horlick along with those of several of their children.

For many years James Horlick served as an official of his township, both in the House of Parliament, and as High Sheriff. He also served as an officer of his church parish. In memory of their parents, James and Priscilla, James and William Horlick donated a marble plaque to St. John the Baptist. It hangs on a church wall and begins with the words "As a tribute of affection..." It is interesting to note that when James Horlick died, he left his estate to sons, James and Peter. The will written on August 14, 1874, does not name son William as an inheritor, just as the will of William's father-in-law, Joseph Alexander Horlick, had not named daughter Arabella as an inheritor. Why neither William nor Arabella (Horlick) Horlick were granted an inheritance from their fathers will likely remain unknown.

St. John The Baptist Church—Ruardean, England
taken by the author

At what point in their lives James and William began to experiment with the idea of developing a mash of malted barley, wheat, flour, and cow's milk, referred to as wort, may never be ascertained either. Certainly it was before their departure to America. Had they worked on the formula at the granary in Ruardean? Did they experiment with a dehydration process that would then allow the wort to be mixed with water thus creating an infant drink free from the possible contamination of milk? Some believe that a copper vessel called a Bain-

Marie was used by the Horlick brothers in their initial attempts to secure a working formula. The Bain-Marie prevented milk poured into it from boiling which would cause the milk to be ruined. Instead, the Bain-Marie kept the liquid in a temperature-controlled vacuum allowing the water to evaporate from the milk, the result being a milk powder.

Like other aspects of this story, there is conflicting information on where the idea for an infant food formula originated, exactly how each step in the process was carried out, and whether it was James or William who, in certain instances, deserved credit for their success. Here is what we do know.

Of the nine children born to James and Priscilla Horlick, only three sons survived. They were Peter, born in 1842, James, born in 1844, and William, born in 1846. All three began their formal education in Ruardean. Later they were sent to a private boarding school at Candover near Hampshire, about ten miles from Winchester.

When the time came, Uncle Nockells Horlick found work for James with a homeopathic chemist named Keene on Bond Street in London. William was apprenticed to a Mr. Owen on Lisle Street in London, where he honed the saddle making skills learned from his father.

Brother Peter returned to Ruardean where he supported himself as both a farmer and a rope maker. Working out of his boyhood home, Peter would lay out the ropes he was making along a corridor that ran the length of the house. (The door on the right in the photo of the Horlick House.) Local legend has it that Peter was the only person in Ruardean who could chuck a coin over the roof of St. John's Church where his family prayed and where many Horlicks lay buried. Years later, "horse and pair" carriages would arrive at Peter Horlick's home laden with gifts and money and liquor. They were sent by James and William, who likewise never forgot the nanny that had once cared for the three Horlick boys. Residing at Foley House until her death at the age of 94, Nanny Jones was still remembered with packages of the products that had brought two of her charges such immense bounty.

Margo Drummond

II. ON THE GROUND AND RUNNING

What motivates anyone to explore, invent, take risks, create? Often it has something to do with childhood. Some have surmised that the profound effect of having lost four of their six brothers and sisters between the ages of two and eight to death was what motivated James and William Horlick in their quest for a wholesome infant food formula. That, of course, is conjecture. For whatever their reasons, the young brothers were about to propel themselves into a life filled with all the elements so often attributed to success, beginning with that of being willing to take risks.

After four years of apprenticeship, William Horlick returned to Gloucestershire where he opened not one but three saddle making shops. Having decided not to go into business with his father, William established himself in a nearby village as well as in Cindeford and in Ross. Understanding early on the value of name recognition in the marketing of a product, the young man had a sign reading: "William Horlick, Saddlemaker," hung over each of the three sites. Later William would jokingly tell his children that he had developed the original concept of "chain stores."

There was "talk" among the country folk over Horlick's seeming lack of modesty as such things were not yet done. Interestingly, one of the most often attributed qualities later used by others to describe William Horlick, as an entrepreneur and philanthropist, was his modesty. Whatever the judgment, his harness and saddle making found favor among the landed gentry who prized the quality reflected in custom-made saddles fashioned by his skilled hands.

In 1869, at the age of 23, William Horlick sold his shops. That November he sailed from Liverpool for New York aboard the steamship the *City of Washington*. It would seem likely that he was accompanied by his uncle, Joseph Alexander Horlick, given the fact that the elder Horlick was known to make regular trips back and forth to England for family visits. Joseph Alexander Horlick is listed as having been born in England on September 26, 1811, and baptized on July 4, 1813, in Cranham. An affidavit included with his will states that he was a British subject and that "his domicile of origin was English."

Whether traveling alone or with his uncle, William Horlick arrived in New York and from there took a train to Chicago. A story passed on to his children told of a nearly penniless William Horlick with but 50 cents in his pocket, saddle tools in hand, walking the streets of the Windy City in search of a job. Meanwhile brother James continued to work as a chemist in London. His employer was the Mellin Company, a manufacturer of baby food.

Now the hard part—beginning with where the original infant food formula that would bring James and William back together in Chicago actually came from. Had the brothers begun to formulate it while in Ruardean, or did James conceive the idea while working for the Mellins? Most probably it was a combination of the two, perhaps influenced by knowledge of malting gleaned from their grandfather Peter and other malters back in Ruardean.

There is another possibility, one offered by a gentleman named W. Pinching in a letter dated March of 1951. According to Mr. Pinching, it was his uncle John Pinching who shared a family recipe for malted milk with the Horlicks, a recipe "taken from an old manuscript Cooking Book" written by successive Pinching wives. Having tried out the recipe himself, John Pinching passed it on to the Horlicks with the prediction that it would make them a fortune. According to Mr. Pinching's account, a member of the Horlick family later informed his father that the Recipe was quite correct but required more sugar in order to please the modern palate. It is worth noting that the Pinching family had settled in Cranham (where grandfather Peter Horlick lived during his youth) sometime around 1660, having been driven from their home at Brimpsfield Park by civil war, and that the Pinchings and the Horlicks were cousins.

Along with the question of where the Horlick formula came from is that of why it was taken to America. James Horlick was thought to be dissatisfied with his work as a chemist in London. Numerous articles credit William with convincing brother James to join him in America where together they could perfect their formula. A theory put forth by some is that patent problems would have prevented the Horlicks from succeeding with their plans in England, given that James was employed by an infant food concern. Mellin Company produced Liebeg Extract, an infant dried food of malt and bran named for a German inventor, Liebeg, who a decade earlier had worked on the process of vacuum drying and concentration of food products. By some accounts, James could not raise the necessary funds in England to market and produce a new drink, and that is why he decided to join brother William in Chicago.

In a letter written by Clifford J. Harrison of Horlick's Limited, Slough-Buckinghamshire, on November 8, 1954, Mr. Harrison responds to an inquiry by a William G. Knight, Esquire, as to the possibility that it was Joseph Alexander Horlick, uncle to James and William, who first came into possession of the formula (as claimed by the Pinchings who said they had passed it on to their cousins, the Horlicks, while both families still resided in Cranham). The response from Mr. Harrison of Horlick's Limited to Mr. Knight was a resounding "No." Wrote Mr. Harrison:

> *The facts are that the original product was called Horlick's Food. It was evolved by James Horlick, later Sir James Horlick, Baronet, who was a chemist and he had the formula for this product before he left England in the early 1870's. Arrived in America he invited his brother, William Horlick, to join him in the venture of the manufacture of Horlick's Food, and they actually started in Chicago, later moving to Racine where they opened the first works in 1873. William Horlick was a stone mason and engineer—he had no knowledge of chemistry.*

A newspaper series published in Wisconsin following the death of William Horlick described efforts by him and Arabella to nail down a formula while they were both still living with her parents in Mt. Pleasant. The story goes on to say that when the couple moved to Chicago following their wedding, the work continued with Arabella cooking up batches during the day while William ran his father-in-law's lime and stone business, and that at night they would work together. When they finally had what they wanted, William would go door to door, building up a customer base by sharing the product with friends and neighbors who had infants or toddlers. As word got out of its positive benefits, demand led to sales that kept Arabella busy preparing bottles of the formula which William could take to customers each evening.

Is it possible that the formula was actually in the hands of Arabella's father, Joseph Alexander Horlick, even before William arrived on the scene? According to the letter written by W. Pinching (March 1951),

> *the Horlicks who emigrated to the USA left England in the middle of the last century. They were much "under the wind" and for some time before they left were put up by our cousin, William Pinching VI, at Ivy Farm Birdlip. They went to Wisconsin, then a frontier town, and had a very poor farm, but it was limestone which as Wisconsin grew became valuable. Later the family took up the malted milk business.*

Joseph Alexander Horlick
courtesy Racine Heritage Museum

This information, if accurate, would refer not to James or William Horlick, but rather to their uncle, Joseph Alexander Horlick. If so, it would explain the story of William and Arabella's work on the formula during the time he was courting her while employed at her father's lime and stone quarry in Mt. Pleasant.

Despite the confusion over whether it was William, who in 1873, urged James to come to Chicago, or, as in other reporting, that James invited William to assist him, the brothers joined forces to create "Horlick's Food for Infants and Invalids" marketed by J and W Horlick Company of Chicago. The original Horlick's Food was the result of drying into powdered form the liquids obtained from macerating wheat, flour, and malted barley with water, resulting in the starch of the flour being converted into maltrose and dextrines. Due to an increasing need for more space, the Horlick brothers moved their operation out of William's home and into an area they leased for $500 a year on Chicago's LaSalle Street. Horlick's, whatever the truth behind its formulation, was "on the ground and running."

Margo Drummond

III. TO WISCONSIN

By 1877 the need for even more space prompted brothers James and William to relocate once again. Familiar with the area north of Chicago, encompassing Racine and Mt. Pleasant, William had earlier purchased eleven acres of farmland there. And so it was on to Wisconsin that James and William ventured.

At a site located on one of the eleven acres of land (some accounts say ten) belonging to William, the Horlick brothers built a modest frame structure measuring twenty by eighty feet with eight ovens and eight chimneys. A boiler, two coppers, as the vacuum pans were called, a mill, a mash tun and a steam engine of the "Corliss" type with belt drives for the various pieces of machinery could be found inside. Canadian-style heating facilities, suited to cold Wisconsin winters were also installed. Years later the brothers would recall how they were forced to stuff newspapers between the floorboards as winter winds whipped across the ground, blowing snow up between the wooden planks that constituted the factory floor.

Original Horlick's Food Company Factory—Racine, Wisconsin
courtesy Racine Heritage Museum

29

The site chosen by James and William Horlick for their factory was selected for its proximity to an abundance of natural springs. Known to and frequented by early Native American inhabitants of the region, the springs bubbled up year round through layers of quicksand, below which were beds of blue clay. Thanks to the work of the glaciers centuries before, southeastern Wisconsin lies in what is known as the artesian water belt. Artesian wells contain salt and mineral-rich water. Two of those artesian wells, one 1,500 feet deep and the other 1,800 feet in depth, provided the mineral-rich water needed by the Horlicks for making their infant formula. Rather than adding mineral salts to the malted mixture, the artesian water was used to guard against their leaking away during the malting process.

In addition to artesian well water, the Horlick formula incorporated large amounts of barley. According to the USDA (United States Department of Agriculture), barley grown in the upper Mississippi region, including Wisconsin, has a high content of nitrogen, important to the process of malting. Additionally, the high enzymatic efficiency of barley, through the enzymes it produces, aids in the process of digestion.

The finished product, patented by the Horlick brothers while still in Chicago in 1873, consisted of a dry, rust-colored substance with the texture of rusk. This "rusk" was finely ground into powder and placed in bottles of either seven or fourteen ounces. According to handwritten ledgers kept by William, seven-ounce bottles were priced at $4.05 per dozen. Fourteen-ounce bottles invoiced at $8.10 per dozen, retailed at about a dollar each. Ingredients necessary for the production included malted barley at 85 cents per bushel, and flour at $2 per quarter. Milk was listed at costing 8 cents per gallon. The Horlicks paid adult labor a dollar per day, maximum, and youngsters half that amount. James and William each drew a salary of $600 per annum. James is shown as having paid $2.35 for a coat and vest while William spent $15.50 on a gun and horn of shot. For purposes of local travel the brothers employed a buggy and for longer trips they traveled by rail, paying $20 for a distance of 2,000 miles.

Horlick's Food Company was incorporated on January 24, 1883. One hundred shares of stock valued at $100 each were issued, 45 of them to James who was made president and 45 to William who was named secretary-treasurer. James' wife, Margaret Adelaide (Burford) Horlick, whom he had married at Westminster, England, in 1873, was awarded five shares of stock as was Arabella Roselia (Horlick) Horlick, William's wife. In 1885 Horlick's Food Company was incorporated in the state of Wisconsin, this time naming Arabella Horlick as a vice president. Company records from the year 1883 show William Horlick earning a salary of $8,000.

William and Arabella lived in a two-story frame house on the grounds of the factory facility, along with three of their four children. Mabelle (birth name Emma Mabel) was born there on April 15, 1877, the same year that her father and uncle built their first factory. Her two older brothers, Alexander James (later known as A.J.) and William, Jr. had been born while their parents still lived in Chicago. The oldest Horlick child, Alice Priscilla, born at Ross Herfordshire, England, on August 10, 1871, died of a convulsion, leading to a fall. Eleven years old at the time of her death, Alice's brief life would be memorialized by her family through generous gifts to the city of Racine in the years that followed.

James and Margaret Horlick, meanwhile, had moved to Brooklyn, New York, where James continued to increase and expand company sales. Their oldest son, Ernest Burford Horlick, had been born in Racine on February 29, 1880. While living in New York, James and Margaret Horlick became the parents of two more sons, James Nockells Horlick, born in Brooklyn on March 22, 1886, and Gerald Nolekin Horlick, born February 1, 1888. The Racine City Directory of 1890 lists James' address as the Merchants Hotel at 423-425 Main St., Racine, perhaps where he stayed during visits back to the Wisconsin facility.

While residing in Brooklyn, James Horlick frequently traveled to Canada and along the northeastern corridor of the United States, convincing druggists and doctors of the worthiness of Horlick's Food as a healthy, nutritious dietary aid, particularly for invalids and infants. At some of the gatherings he attended, James was confronted by physicians concerned about the fact that sterile milk was necessary to prepare his product for use. In those days fresh sterile milk was not always available, especially in warmer climates, and the idea of pasteurization through boiling away bacteria had not yet taken off in America. With infant mortality rates as high as they were, a solution to the problem of contaminated milk needed to be found.

On June 5, 1893, Patent #278967 was issued to William Horlick. For some time he and Arabella had been working to solve the problem of adding purified milk to the Horlick's infant formula. Over and over again William was quoted as having said to his wife, "Arabella, we have to get pure milk into our product if we ever hope to save lives wholesale." According to a long-time Horlick employee, the deed was finally accomplished as follows.

First, malted barley and wheat flour were combined. To that mixture was added water, forming a mash, a sticky, gooey, brown substance. The mash was then cooked gently with steam until the enzymes in the barley malt changed the starches to sugar. Rich whole milk was then added to the barley mixture and cooked in two stages on a vacuum to reduce the moisture. Air was pumped away so that the boiling could take place at a low temperature of about 140 degrees so as not to harm the material. When the material contained approximately three percent moisture, solidification took place. The result was a very chunky porous sponge-like material which when reduced to powder form became known as malted milk. It is believed that William and Arabella Horlick were assisted in formulating the malted milk process by Dr. F. J. Pope and Professor Robert Hindley.

Some reports indicate that James Horlick was not initially convinced that changes to their product were a good idea since they might adversely affect the growing sales he had managed to generate. But according to a letter written by Mr. Clifford J. Harrison of Horlick's Limited (Slough, England) in November of 1954, what James Horlick really objected to was not being able to keep the malted milk formula a secret should it be patented. Against his wishes, brother William took out the patent while James was in England, thus opening the formula to scrutiny. At that time, James was working with a German pharmacist, Oscar Kress, and a salesman named Samuel Owens who originally had been half-owner of a drugstore in Racine. Owens had traveled the southern United States selling Horlick's before relocating to New York where lucrative commissions had lured him.

While his name does not appear on the 1893 patent, James Horlick did, in the end, contribute his share of $3,000 toward production and patent costs initially financed by his brother. The money may have been borrowed from Oscar Kress. Neither Kress nor Owen was happy to learn that, by 1890, James Horlick had decided to move back to England. However, with the capital they had garnered from the success of Horlick's, the two went on to develop another world-renowned product, Glyco-thymoline.

The term "malted milk" was not patented until 1887. In June of that same year it was introduced as a health food at the AMA (American Medical Association) Conference in Chicago. Carrying a large case of free samples, William Horlick gathered crowds of doctors about him as he attempted to persuade them of the necessity for pure milk in the diets of infants and invalids.

At some point during his presentation, Mr. Horlick was asked to leave by Dr. N.S. Davis of Chicago who, as president of the association, was struggling to get his fellow physicians' attention. After having asked a second time, Dr. Davis shouted at Horlick and gave him a shove. With that, the 42-year-old Horlick, an athlete and amateur boxer, rolled up his sleeves saying, "Touch me again and I'll knock you out." Horlick then removed himself and his products to a hallway outside the auditorium where he continued to attract crowds. In later years Mr. Horlick and Dr. Davis became friends who delighted in recounting the story of their near altercation. Meanwhile, sales of malted milk skyrocketed both in America and in England. An exhibit at the Chicago World's Fair that same summer only added to its notoriety. The time had come, it seemed, for Horlick's to go global.

Lewis and Clark World's Fair, Portland, Oregon (circa 1906)
courtesy Clem Krivich

IV. GOING GLOBAL

Going global meant changes of great magnitude for both James and William Horlick. In 1890 James had moved with his family back to England, setting up an office at 39 Snow Hill Road, Holborn, London. From there he could better focus upon the growing British and European markets. The first order taken for Horlick's by James from that office was to supply Fortnum and Mason, the well-known grocers of Piccadilly.

Horlick's Malted Milk Factory—Racine, Wisconsin
courtesy Racine Heritage Museum

William, meanwhile, had focused his attention on the construction of a new factory in Racine, Wisconsin. Grand in design and scale, the structure bore a striking resemblance to castles found in the Horlicks' native England. Three cream-colored brick buildings would eventually rise from thick stone foundations along with a four-story, 35,000 square foot tower housing the largest three-sided clock in the state. Underground tunnels connected the entirety. A simple sketch drawn by Mr. Horlick himself was all that James Corse and Sons had to follow in constructing Building Number One. The tower theme utilized in the first unit would later be carried out in those that followed. Altogether, the factory would eventually encompass almost 500,000 square feet, Plant Number Two having been built in 1902, followed by Plant Number Three just three years later.

During a visit to Racine, Henry Bacon, who had designed the Lincoln Memorial in Washington, D.C., described the Horlick facility as one of the most beautiful he had ever seen. With its ivy-covered walls, cobblestoned courtyards, and meticulous landscaping complete with an artificial lake graced by Australian swans, the site more nearly resembled a park than a place of production.

Grounds and Swan Pond of Horlick Factory—Racine, Wisconsin
courtesy Racine Heritage Museum

The London offices of Horlick's, managed by James, had meanwhile been relocated to 34 Farringdon Road. From there James Horlick successfully marketed Horlick products throughout the world. Richard Preston, who had been trained in Racine, was sent over to supervise the depot at Farringdon Road, the agreement being that America would supply goods at 10 percent over cost and then whatever profit the English depot produced would be shared 50-50 by the Horlick brothers.

Thanks in large part to the efforts of James and his staff, by the early 1900's Horlick's had become a product of the world. Mr. Horlick personally appointed salesmen and agents, chosen from those he met during his extensive travels. Exports of Horlick products could be found in such faraway places as Australia, New Zealand, China, Burma, India, Ceylon and Malaysia. Advertising for Horlick's in England included such creative concepts as life-sized cutout cows placed in fields along major railroad lines and labeled, "Horlick's Malted Milk." Ads also began to appear in English newspapers including *The Daily Mail, The Daily Telegraph*, and *The Times of London.*

Advertisements for Horlick's included its use as: a builder of sound teeth, a comfort following anesthesia, a panacea for ulceration or neuralgia, an aid to nursing mothers, as well as a convenient source of nourishment to travellers, sportsmen, growing children, invalids, and office workers with a limited lunch break.

In America the Horlicks employed over 100 telephone operators who made nationwide calls offering free samples of their products. They likewise sent out letters of advertisement such as this one from September of 1927: (Please turn to next page.)

May we mail you, free of cost, for trial at your home, a sample of Horlick's, the Original Malted Milk?

With "Horlick's" on hand, a delicious Food-Drink may be prepared instantly, day or night, which is both satisfying and invigorating, and unlike many table drinks, does not affect the nerves or digestion. As a light lunch at any time, it relieves hunger and fatigue. It upbuilds the convalescent, and those who are "run down". A cupful, taken hot upon retiring, is conducive to sound, refreshing sleep.

Horlick's Malted Milk is far superior to ordinary cow's milk, whether for infants, growing children or adults, since it contains, in addition to rich, full-cream milk, all the valuable food-constituents, including the vitamins and mineral elements, of wheat and barley. The extracts of these grains also have a modifying effect upon the milk when subjected to our special process, making the milk, with the additions, much more nutritious and more easily assimilable.

"Horlick's" needs no cooking, being prepared by briskly stirring the powder in a little hot or cold water, gradually adding the desired quantity of water or plain milk. The use of a mixer or an eggbeater brings out the delicious aroma, and instantly produces a well-aerated refreshing drink. (Our Speedy Mixer is very handy, and will be sent you by mail for the nominal price of 10¢ in coin or stamps.

We suggest, in order that you may obtain the valuable constituents as well as the real Malted Milk flavor of the Original, that you specify "Horlick's" and thus avoid imitations and adulterants.

We enclose a blank form for your convenience in applying for a free trial package.   Very truly yours,

CT   HORLICK'S MALTED MILK CORPORATION.

Horlick Malted Milk Advertisement—September 1927
Racine, Wisconsin

One Horlick employee (who recently died at the age of 99) attributed her lifelong wanderlust and penchant for travels to exotic locales as harkening back to the time when she was addressing letters to such places, places a young woman working at the Horlick factory in Racine could only dream of. Another recalled being part of a group of 28 girls who sat around a table placing seals and covers on jars of malted milk and malted milk tablets. Often times Mr. Horlick would pass by with his neatly trimmed trademark goatee and silver-headed cane.

Despite or perhaps because of their seemingly unstoppable success, the Horlick brothers began to differ on where to go next. William wanted to purchase a factory site near Montreal in Canada, an idea deemed "not agreeable," by James. Instead, James was pushing for construction of a plant in Slough (rhymes with cow), England, just across the Thames River from Windsor.

"I have not agreed to the Slough purchase," William telegraphed James, to which James replied, "I am surprised and thought we had agreed as my sons do not want to waste the rest of their lives in old offices at 34 Farringdon Road." For his part, William argued that should a factory be built at Slough, it should only be for bottling and not for manufacturing, stressing that the English side of production was not yet well enough established.

On May 3, 1906, James wrote to William saying, "I wish we had built the factory here instead of Racine, but no good talking about that." At the end of that same month, James again wrote to William stating his objection to a Canadian factory which he deemed, "too expensive and not enough sales." A series of cables which the brothers exchanged during the summer months of 1906 indicate tension over who would prevail regarding a Canadian facility versus one in England.

Potential plans for a factory at Slough had been drawn up by A.J. Christiansen, a Racine-based engineer, sent to England to determine approximate costs for such a project and referred to in the following cablegram: (Please turn to next page.)

Racine Wis, June 7th 06.

My dear James,

        I recd your cablegram "Not agreeable" a few
days ago and of course understood same to mean that you
were <u>not agreeable</u> to the proposition I submitted to you
regarding the purchasing of a factory site for our Company
near Montreal Canada if same could be obtained at a reasonable
figure and as more fully explained in my letter to you on
May 17th last.

        Wm Jr handed a letter to me which he recd from Mr
Christainsen two days ago under date May 25th said letter
containing an approximate cost for new ractory building
for the Company at Slough.   I was very astonished when I
read the paragraph at the bottom of first page of his
letter which reads as follows " I am sorry to state I
have not been able to commence the building as the siding
has not yet been commenced &c &c "   This is all the
more astonishing as he distinctly understood from me when
here that I should want to approve of the Plans and cost
for building a Factory in England berore our Company became
obligated. Moreover I have expressed the same desire to
you frequently and as contained in my letter to you of
May 17th previously rererred to, hence my reason for cabling
you yesterday as follows;- "Dont build factory until plans
and cost approved here" to which I recd cable reply from
you today Bgave you estimates and plans cannot delay
without serious increase expenses" to which I now cable
reply " I have not approved plans and cost Dont build
until I do"

        It is obvious in order to avoid any difficulties

that we should be in perfect accord before our Company
becomes involved in a heavy building expenditure. I regret
if this delay should cause you any serious increase expense
but it is evident it is no fault of mine and by next mail
I will give my views regarding the costs submitted.

x   x   ^   x

Your affectionate Brother

William.

One of Two Cablegrams—Exchanged by James and William Horlick—1906
courtesy Horlick Museum, Slough, England

The following day, June 8, 1906, a purchase of 6½ acres of land at a cost of 600 pounds per acre was made in Slough. In a cablegram sent by James to William, James acknowledged the receipt of William's share of the cost of that purchase, sent from the National Bank in Chicago.

On June 11, William wrote back to James reiterating past and current objections to the Slough facility moving forward without further consultation: (Please turn to next page.)

Racine Wis, June 11th 1906.

My dear James,

I am in receipt of your letter of May 31st and not what you say in regard to the idea of our purchasing a site for a factory in Canada near Montreal if same could be had particulars of which were given you in my letter of May 17th last. As stated to you in my letter of June 7th we will let the matter drop seeing that you are not agreeable to the project.

In my letter to you of June 7th I stated that I was very much astonished when I read in Mr Christainsen's letter to Wm Jr under date of May 25th last and for the first time learned that you were apparently seriously considering the work of building our factory before even submitting even proper plans estimates etc to me for my approval or even before the Railway siding has been put in to the property all of which you know has been distinctly understood between us as also with Mr Christainsen in discussing matters when here hence my reason for sending the recent cables to you asking you not to build until I had approved plans cost etc etc Consequently I was I might say astounded when I read in your letter of May 31st recd today that the boilers girders and brick were ordered and flooring practically so.

You have not informed me personally at all in regard to this contemplated serious expenditure. Neither has any attention apparently been given to my letters of November 29th 1905 January 18th 1906 Febry 8th 1906 Febry 19th 1906 May 14th 1906 May 17th 1906.

It would seem to me that it would be better for us to come to an understanding on this matter and so avoid the possibility of any further difficulty.

           x   x Yr affte Bro
                                    Wm Horlick.

One of Two Cablegrams—Exchanged by James and William Horlick—1906
courtesy Horlick Museum, Slough, England

Eventually, William gave in to James. Perhaps a change of heart occurred when James reminded William that he had not been consulted over construction costs at the Racine operation some years before.

Within two years, a building looking remarkably similar to the one in Racine arose in Slough. Situated along the railroad siding, it was made of red, rather than cream-colored brick. The mechanical engineer named A.G. Christiansen was sent to America for consultation with the Racine operation before returning to England where he would oversee the project. He made the journey for twenty pounds, traveling second class. The Slough factory was completed in 1908 at a cost of 28,000 British pounds.

Horlick's Factory—Slough, England
taken by the author

Those years leading up to World War I were perhaps some of the best Horlick's would ever know. Due to ingenious advertising campaigns and savvy marketing techniques, sales both in America and abroad continued to climb. James and William Horlick had once joked that if their incomes ever exceeded $60,000 annually they would have "reached the limit." Some years after making that statement, their gross was in the millions with one year's advertising costing more than a million dollars.

There was certainly enough money to go around as members of the second generation began to work for the company. As James pointed out to William, England was "paying its fair share," which it was. Another of the arguments that James Horlick had used to persuade his brother, William, as to the need for a factory in Slough was that his sons could become involved in the family business, which they did. William's sons, A.J. and William, Jr., had likewise joined the company, A.J. in marketing and William, Jr., an itinerant inventor and trained engineer, in production.

In 1894, A.J. Horlick attended the first official American Medical Association Convention in order to further enhance the company's market shares, a task made easier thanks to the groundwork laid by James and William years before. A.J.'s pitch, similar to the one used by his father and uncle, emphasized the purity of powdered milk so basic to the Horlick product. Four years earlier, the Horlicks had established their own dairy farms in Wisconsin to ensure that the milk they used in their "perfect food product" was as pure and fresh as the milkmaids displayed in much of their advertising, each milkmaid often shown standing in a field of flowers beside a picture-perfect cow.

Milk, now a key component of the Horlick formula, had become renowned for its purity based on strict standards of production practiced at the Horlick dairy barns. A lengthy document entitled, "Horlick's Malted Milk Company Milk Regulations" detailed those guidelines and standards. Barns were to be located away from possible contaminants, well lighted and heated, spacious and free from dust and/or manure. Cows were to be fed on clover and barley, kept free from flies and never milked while infected. Barn workers at the farms were required to dress in white uniforms. The milk delivered to the plant on Northwestern Avenue in Racine was guaranteed to have been taken early and properly handled enroute with only certain utensils used in each step of the process. Such standards ultimately raised those reportedly used by dairy farms across the state and served as a prototype for dairy barns at the University of Wisconsin. There were five Horlick dairy farms in all, the largest encompassing about 500 acres. Designated as Farm Number One, it stretched from High Street to South Street to the site of Horlick (now Batten) Airfield, including the land on which William Horlick High School would eventually be built. That farm was managed by a Danish immigrant named Max Clemmensen who was encouraged by Mr. Horlick to recruit other Danes to come to America for work at the Horlick dairy farms.

Clemmensen's daughter recalled visits made to the farm by Mr. Horlick in his chauffeur-driven car. On one such visit he presented the little girl with the gift of a beautiful doll. On another he gave her father, a loyal employee of 33 years, the cutter Horlick himself had once used. Along with the cutter came Beauty, a retired racehorse whose reins were studded with ruby-colored stones.

Horlick Dairy Cows
courtesy Racine Heritage Museum

Horlick's gift was well deserved by Max Clemmensen whose ten-hour days began at 4:30 a.m. when he would see to it that the 100 black and white Holsteins under his care were milked and fed according to a strictly adhered to schedule. Calling each cow by a name he had personally given them, Clemmensen and his five hands would then groom the animals, housed in barns that were freshly whitewashed each spring.

So well treated were the cows by Mr. Clemmensen that when he was away in Iowa for a week, they dropped 33 percent of their milk production. That occurred, despite the fact that they were fed barley grown on the farm along with mash left over from plant production. Pigs raised on Farm Number One were also pampered with regular feedings of malted milk tablets. And in the fall, as Russet and Northern Spry apples fell from trees in the orchard, sheep and lambs (some destined for the Horlick dining table) were allowed to fatten up by feasting on the fruit.

In 1951, the remaining Horlick dairy herd, comprised of 68 Holsteins, was sold. Of the five original Horlick dairy farms, all that remained were some 350 acres. Once part of Farm Number One, that last parcel was turned over to the Horlick Investment Company, under management of O.E. Rennic.

In 1912, to further insure their reputation as a safe and nutritious infant food, the Horlick's Malted Milk Company circulated a 30-page pamphlet for mothers, providing them with information not only about the general care and feeding of babies, but about how their product could aid in that process. The brochure recommended that children be kept largely on Horlick's Malted Milk until well into their second year. Featured in the materials were pictures of healthy "Horlick babies." Sales that year topped the three million dollar mark with 16-17 percent of that amount having been spent on advertising

Horlick's Malted Milk, one advertisement stated:

supplies all the elements of nutrition necessary to sustain life single handed, hence its great value in adult cases. It is being administered as a diet with excellent results in Typhoid and other low fevers as well as in all Gastric,

Intestinal and Bronchial difficulties. It is retained by the most delicate stomach after all other foods fail. It is a boon to nursing mothers, delicate women, invalids, and convalescents generally. A glass taken hot upon retiring is almost a specific in insomnia. It is a most excellent substitute for tea, coffee, cocoa, beef tea, etc., as its stimulating and nourishing effects are lasting.

Certainly what the Horlicks touted as far as quality of product could not easily be refuted. At a farm owned by a Danish family named Sorenson outside Racine, it was not unusual to find William Horlick, there to select the finest wheat and barley available for use at his factory. A son of the Sorenson family who grew up on that farm remembered seeing Mr. Horlick, seated in the back of an open, chauffeur-driven car, dressed in a fur-collared coat, much as Max Clemmensen's daughter remembered him on his visits to the dairy farm.

Such quality control obviously paid off. A photograph of Theodore Roosevelt standing in front of boxes of Horlick's as he began his South American exploration of the River of Doubt in 1913 attests to that. William Horlick, an unquestionable believer in and supporter of world exploration, gave generously to such causes, including that of Admiral Richard E. Perry's polar expeditions of 1908-1909. Horlick products, cash and gifts were bestowed upon Norwegian explorer Roald Amundsen before and after his journey to the South Pole in 1910-1911. A cable sent to Horlick by Amundsen read: "the way straight to the Pole is now littered with empty boxes stamped, "Horlick's Racine.""

In September of 1913 Mr. Horlick made a gift to Amundsen of a gold compass inscribed, "To Explorer Roald Amundsen from the House of Horlick." It was meant to be taken on Amundsen's next planned exploration to the North Pole. Other gifts to Amundsen included a valuable thermometer and barometer as well as supplies of Horlick's shipped at company expense in whatever quantities desired. There was also a cash gift of $7,500.

Having likely met at a dinner given in honor of Captain

Amundsen at the Scandinavian Club in Milwaukee in February of 1913, the two remained friends throughout their lifetimes. Amundsen visited the Horlicks in Racine on at least two occasions, once in 1918 and again in 1924. Known as an eccentric, Amundsen had been scheduled to deliver talks in six American cities. Asked why he failed to show up for all but two, the explorer replied that there were only two cities that interested him, one being Racine where his friend, William Horlick, lived.

Horlick's support of Norwegian explorers and scientists was duly rewarded. In 1922, His Majesty King Haakon of Norway made Mr. Horlick a Knight of the Order of St. Olaf of the first class. Requests by his friends for a celebration of that auspicious occasion were denied by the ever self-effacing and modest Mr. Horlick who expressed doubts over whether he should rightfully accept the honor at all.

In 1914, brother James had been made a baronet by King George V of England, conferring upon him the title of Sir James. That title was eventually passed down to his son Ernest (and upon his death) to brother James, who discounted its significance as nothing but a holdover from English history when King James I, desperately in need of cash, had created the title system as a means of raising revenue.

That the lives and good fortunes of James and William Horlick seemed to parallel one another during the years leading up to World War I was vividly reflected in an incident which occurred during April of 1906. William and Arabella Horlick had embarked on a business and pleasure trip to California. While visiting in San Francisco, the great earthquake struck, leaving the couple badly jarred but basically without injury. At the same time, James was yachting along the coast of Italy as a guest of shipping tycoon Sir Charles Furness. While refueling in the port of Naples, the volcano Vesuvius erupted, spewing a shower of fine ash that James likened to "a Wisconsin snowstorm." But as with his brother and sister-in-law who were half a world away, James Horlick, while shaken, escaped unharmed.

V. PRIVATE LIVES

In 1906, shortly before work on the factory at Slough was begun, James Horlick purchased an 1,870 acre estate not far from Cheltenham known as Cowley Manor. Originally built in 1695, the house had undergone several renovations but none perhaps as extensive as that undertaken by R.A. Briggs for Mr. Horlick. The main block of the house was doubled in size, six bay windows were added along with a piazza across the front, which included an extremely ornamental shell-roofed doorway. The dining room was expanded to measure 42 by 23 feet. Also added were a billiards room, a garden hall, a conservatory, a pavilion, a ballroom measuring 65 by 31 feet, large enough to accommodate 400 people, along with eighteen new bedrooms. Leading up to the bedrooms was a grand staircase. The second floor halls and corridors formed a picture gallery. One beautifully decorated boudoir that remained after the house had been renovated reflected the craftsmanship of foreign workmen, imported by a previous owner 50 years before.

Cowley Manor—Gloucestershire, England
courtesy Sir John Horlick

49

The finest English craftsmen available were engaged to do the plaster work, mahogany paneling and lime-wood ornamentation which included "exquisite festoons and cartouches in pear wood." With the addition of fine Chippendale, Sheraton, and Hepplewhite antique furnishings, along with Worcester and Chelsea china, Cowley Manor became known as "the most grand and richly decorated house in Gloucestershire." Adding to the overall charm of the house was the fact that it was filled with vases of fresh flowers, especially roses, and that in the background could be heard the constant chattering of exotic birds such as parrots and macaws.

An avid horticulturist, Mr. Horlick was said to have had 700,000 trees planted on the grounds of his estate, which also included elaborate gardens behind the house, as well as a series of terraces connected by stone steps leading down to a water garden comprised of an upper and lower lake, each complemented by statuary and fountains. On the lake were Australian swans, which interestingly were also found on the lagoon of the William Horlick property in America—a fact that becomes

Cascade of Cowley Manor
courtesy Sir John Horlick

more meaningful toward the end of this story. Looking west through the Ionic colonade that opened from the picture gallery and other reception rooms of Cowley Manor was a view of woods and hills, green pastures, rippling waters, and, in the valley below, one of seven springs which form the source of the River Thames.

As president of the Gloucestershire Agricultural Society along with the Gloucestershire Root, Fruit and Grain Society, James Horlick contributed not only beauty but his own impressive knowledge and talents to the area in which he lived. He served as Justice of the Peace for his county in 1900 and afterwards as Deputy Lieutenant. During the coronation year, he was chosen as High Sheriff of Gloucestershire. In the late 1800's, he had cottages built for workers in the nearby village and in 1900 saw to it that the school there was enlarged. The workers who lived there were employed at Cowley Manor as carpenters, kitchen and stable hands, drivers, housekeepers, farmers, and caretakers of the estate's famous herd of shorthorns that could be seen grazing on the park-like slopes opposite the house. "There is little question," noted an article written about Cowley Manor in August of 1906, "that in an English park, cows are more ornamental than deer." True or not, cows and Horlick's Malted Milk were synonymous during those golden years.

When World War I began, all three sons of James and Margaret (Burford) Horlick enlisted. Referring to the title he inherited from his father and brother, James Horlick (while visiting in Racine years later) would declare that there was but one title of which he was most proud, that of being a member of the Old Contemptibles. The Old Contemptibles were members of the British Expeditionary Force during the first two months of the war. Dubbed by German Kaiser Wilhelm as the "Contemptible Little Army," the unit suffered 25,000 casualties during their service to the British cause.

Of the 40 officers who served with him in the trenches, James Horlick was one of only two who survived. He left the service as a Colonel of the Coldstream Guard. His younger brother, Major Gerald Nolekin Horlick, died of malaria at Alexandria, Egypt, on July 5, 1918, while on active service. Gerald's own attempts to keep his comrades in the trenches from succumbing to dysentery by supplying them with Horlick's were reflected in a 1922 memorial to Major Horlick.

James Nockells Horlick returned home from war to marry Flora McDonald Martin from the Scottish Isle of Skye. James and Flora had three children, Katherine, Ursula and John. Katherine married Kenneth Wagg and together they had four sons. Following their divorce, she took up residence in Egypt, leaving him to raise the children with the help of a nanny. He later married the movie actress, Margaret Sullivan, thereafter dividing his time between their home in Greenwich, Connecticut, and his work as president of Horlick's in Racine. Ursula Horlick was married twice, the second time to Colonel John Weaver. Their son, Giles, and John's son, Sir James, still live in the United Kingdom.

James' older brother, Ernest, married Flora's sister, known to the family as Jitty. Ernest and Jitty had two daughters, Roma and Betsan, and a son, Peter. Roma married the Earl of Dartmouth, Betsan died while living in Australia, and Peter, who inherited the title of "sir" from his father, became the father of two girls, Natasha and Anna.

Like their cousins A.J. and William, Jr. in America, the two surviving sons of James Horlick went to work in the family company. When Ernest died in 1934, James took over as president. During the intervening years, James had divided his time between a home near Sunningdale called Little Paddocks and a summer house in Scotland called Greywalls which he had procured in 1924 as a site for enjoying tennis, golf and grouse shooting. Designed by Sir Edwin Luytens in 1901, Greywalls boasted gardens created by England's renowned female landscape architect, Gertrude Jekyll. The property was inherited by James Horlick's daughter, Ursula (Horlick) Weaver and her husband, John. In 1948 they converted it to a hotel which it remains today, overseen by their son, Giles Weaver. Cowley Manor is also now a hotel, as is the former Horlick home at Sunningdale.

Following 18 years as president of Horlick's Malted Milk, James Horlick retired from the company founded by his father and his uncle. During six years of that time, from 1923-1929, he had also served as

Greywalls—Muirfield, Gullane, East Lothian, Scotland
courtesy Giles Weaver

a member of the British Parliament. In 1924 Sir James purchased an island off the coast of Scotland known as Gigha, meaning "God's Island." Measuring six miles by two miles, the grounds at Gigha were forested by Mr. Horlick with some 700,000 trees, just as Cowley Manor had been by his father years before.

To local residents, Sir James was known as a fine and gracious gentleman who made the island viable by raising dairy production to 250,000 gallons of milk per year. It was somewhat ironic that while Sir James was building up the dairy industry on Gigha, the dairy herds established in Racine by his Uncle William during the 1890's were being sold.

At his island home, Achamore House (now also a boutique hotel), ten gardeners were employed to care for the rhododendrons (including Horlick's hybrids) that were Mr. Horlick's passion. Having converted deciduous woods around the house to gardens, he had them filled with not only rhododendrons and bulbs but also with rare species of palm lilies as well as palm and flame trees transplanted from his home in Sunningdale, Ascot. It was because of his extensive knowledge and skill that Sir James was awarded the Victorian Medal of Honor for gardeners, known as the V.M.H.

Achamore House—Horlick's Island Home
courtesy Sir John Horlick

Until his death at Achamore House in 1972, Sir James delighted in touring his gardens in a dragon-caparisoned motorized tricycle. One of the gardens to which he paid regular visits was dedicated to the memory of Malcolm Allen who had served as head gardener for Mr. Horlick for over 50 years. In the island's church there is a stained glass window dedicated to James Nockells Horlick. Below that window, as well as on the sills below other of the church windows, are kept flowering bulbs such as hyacinths and daffodils in memory of the man who beautified the island of Gigha with so many of them. Inhabitants of Gigha bought the island for themselves in 2001

At St. Mary's Church in Elkstone (Gloucester) where James had worshipped as a boy, there can be seen a bronze plaque near the belfry door. It was commissioned by his older brother, Ernest, in 1927 to honor the memory of their parents, James and Margaret, and their brother, Gerald, who died in World War I. Ernest had the old church bells

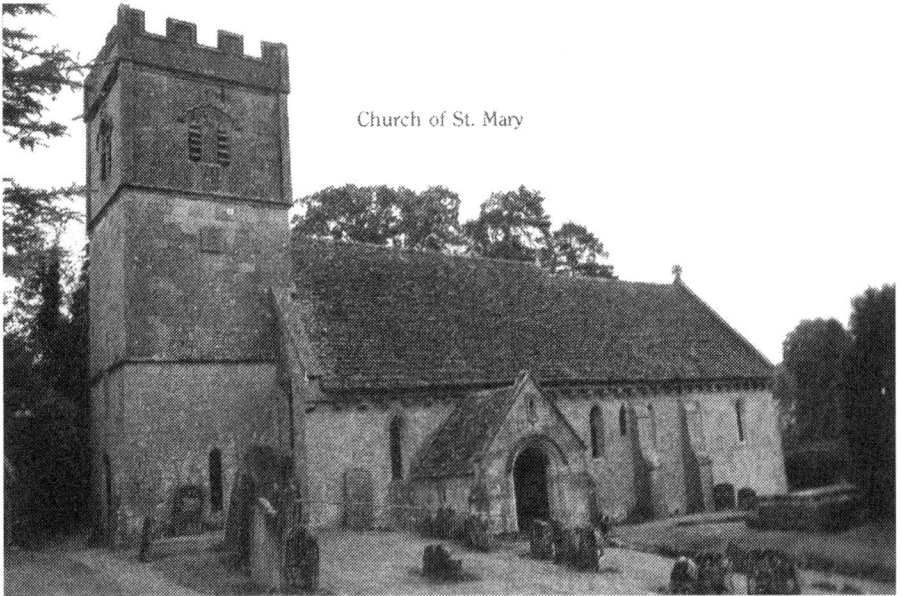
Church of St. Mary

St. Mary's Church, Elkstone (Gloucester), England
courtesy Sir John Horlick

repaired and a new treble bell added, much as his father, James, had done for the cathedral in Ruardean. When he died in 1934, Ernest Burford Horlick was buried alongside his parents and his brother in that chapel, not far from the family estate at Cowley Manor.

The house and grounds occupied by William and Arabella Horlick and their three children would not have been deemed an estate. Their house was a rambling Queen Anne-style structure located on the site of the Horlick's Malted Milk factory in Racine. And while certainly not modest in size, the edifice that William and Arabella Horlick called home had a comfortable, lived-in air to it which may have explained why children who grew up with the Horlick boys, A.J. and William, Jr., later commented that they never really thought of the two young men as "rich."

Most notable about the exterior of the Horlick house at 2220 Northwestern Avenue was a large porte-cochere and a three-story rounded tower, both added during remodeling of the original structure. Striped awnings gave it a summery feeling although Christmas was the favorite holiday of the family. It was then that two enormous evergreens on either side of the entry way gates were festooned with lights. An elk-drawn sleigh was also used to celebrate, the elk having come into the Horlicks' possession following an Elks convention held in Racine sometime before.

Horlick Elk Team at Entrance to Horlick Factory—Racine, Wisconsin
courtesy Gerald Karwowski

Flowers were clearly as important to the American branch of the Horlick family as they were to the British side. An impressive greenhouse stood near the house on Northwestern Avenue, serving as the likely source for the beds of cannas and geranium-filled urns. The property was originally landscaped by a nursery located on Sheridan Road called Green Leaves, owned by a Mr. Macemon. In one old photograph of their gardens, William and Arabella Horlick are shown seated there in wicker chairs, relaxed and smiling as they enjoyed a summer's day together.

Inside the house there were a number of spacious rooms including a foyer, living room, parlor, dining room, kitchen, servants' quarters, and an aviary with a black and white tiled floor. There was also a ballroom for entertaining and a library where it was said Mr. Horlick stored fine wines and jellies of which he kept regular inventories. Perhaps because they chose to remain such private people, little survives in the way of further details. Following the death of his parents, William Horlick, Jr.

William and Arabella Horlick Residence—Racine, Wisconsin
courtesy Racine Heritage Museum

continued to live in his childhood home. Some years after he died, it was demolished and replaced with a filling station.

William Horlick Mansion—Collins Avenue, Miami, Florida
courtesy Gerald Karwowski

57

In 1920 William Horlick paid $200,000 for a lavish Florida mansion and all of its contents. Known as Hanan Hall for its original owner, John R. Hanan, a New York shoe manufacturer, the property occupied 200 feet of ocean front along what was then known as "Millionaire's Row" in Miami. Stretching back 400 feet to Collins Avenue, Hanan House, with its eight bedrooms, was known as one of the largest in the area. Having become acquainted with other people who lived nearby, William Horlick no doubt found time spent in their company an appealing alternative to harsh Wisconsin winters. He often vacationed there with his daughter, Mabelle, who shared in her father's love for baseball, music, and fishing, fishing being an activity that Mabelle and her father had shared in since she was a child.

Mabelle Horlick's birth name was actually Emma Mabel, but for most of her life she was known as Mabelle. Born at the family home in Racine, she was first educated by a private tutor, Elvin Scott. Later she attended the McMynn School in Racine, which was public, followed by Kemper Hall, a private girl's school in Kenosha, Wisconsin, just south of Racine. After that she went to France where she studied voice and piano.

Returning from abroad, she married Dr. John Streeter Sidley whom she had met in Denver, Colorado. An elaborate wedding ceremony was held in Racine on June 30, 1910. Following the receptions given for the couple in both Chicago and New York, they sailed for Europe to begin a year-long honeymoon. Mabelle (Horlick) Sidley's lavish lifestyle was well known and widely publicized. She and her husband inhabited a twelve-acre estate known as "The Oaks," named for the enormous old oak trees that surrounded it. It was located on Washington Avenue (near the corner of Flett) in Racine. Previously, the property had belonged to Charles Erskine, son of one of the "big four" shareholders in the J.I. Case farm implement company which was also located in Racine.

Dr. Sidley, a physician, worked in the medical department at the Horlicks' company. That department was once described by Sidley's brother-in-law, William Horlick, Jr., as a department "in charge of Medical and Professional propaganda." In 1921, Dr. Sidley was elected

"The Oaks"—Home of Mabelle (Horlick) and Dr. John Sidley—Racine, Wisconsin
courtesy Racine Heritage Museum

secretary of the company, an office which he held until his wife's appointment to that post in 1929.

John and Mabelle Sidley often entertained at home. Guests would enter the Sidley mansion through enormous plate-glass doors leading into a foyer whose vaulted ceiling and curving walls were covered with $6,000 of gold leaf. The foyer floor was inlaid marble and on the walls hung priceless tapestries along with medieval armor. A ten-foot wide staircase carpeted in red led up to a balcony and then curved up to the second floor. The balcony was highlighted by a stained glass skylight which cast brilliant color over the music room below.

The library at The Oaks was dominated by a massive black and gold Italian marble fireplace. Three walls of that room had solid walnut bookcases, the fourth wall covered in gold Chinese grasscloth. Glass doors encompassed the entire south side of the living room which opened onto a large screened-in porch tiled in black and white marble. A panel in the living room hid the entrance to a small passageway, at the end of which was a vault where Mrs. Sidley kept many of her precious jewels. On the north wall of the red-tiled dining room were stained glass windows embellished with the Horlick and Sidley family coats-of-arms. The massive chairs at the table in the dining room were covered in striped fur.

Horlick Coat of Arms—"The Oaks"—Racine, Wisconsin
courtesy Sir John Horlick

World-famous artists were frequently included as part of the Sidley guest list. Mrs. Sidley would proudly accompany them to her thirty-foot long music room whose walls and fourteen-foot high ceiling were canvassed for best acoustic effects. North facing windows in the music room were framed by elaborate draperies hung on gold-plated rods, the light fixtures throughout were gold-plated as well. A mirror-paneled passageway leading to the music room concealed hidden compartments for music, phonograph records and instruments. The den was decorated in a Native American motif, replete with Navajo rugs and craftwork. Several pantries and kitchens tiled in bright red linoleum were where the Sidley's household staff prepared for entertaining.

Mrs. Sidley's bedroom was on the second floor of the mansion. Surrounding a white Victorian marble fireplace were walls covered in a richly colorful floral print. The suite included a private dressing room, a bath, and a concealed stairway which led to an enormous sunporch with windows on all four sides. Here among bookcases, window seats, and cupboards could be found the most comfortable room in the house.

From the sunroom one could look out on the grounds of the twelve-acre Sidley estate, unique for its size and location in the heart of the city. A driveway leading past the summer house and tennis courts flanked the Malcolm Erskine property to the east. By crossing a deep bridge-covered ravine, it was possible for liveried chauffeurs to deliver passengers to the mansion. At the west end was the service entrance. It led to garages, above which the Sidley chauffeur lived. At the extreme west end of the estate was a little gardener's cottage.

The Sidleys' only child, William Horlick Sidley, was born in 1912. Described as a lonely and over-protected boy with few playmates, he was often found spending time in the company of a gardener or the chauffeur. Below The Oaks was a park, partially secured for the city by William Horlick. A skater on the park's pond would recall years later having seen young William Horlick Sidley standing behind a fence alone, "watching us skate on the rink." When his parents divorced in 1929, young William chose to leave The Oaks to live with his father. William Horlick Sidley inherited The Oaks from his mother upon her death. Mabelle (Horlick) Sidley's will stated that her only child was to have the house for as long as he chose, after which it was to be given to the Salvation Army. At the time of his induction into the army during World War II, William Horlick Sidley offered the Salvation Army The Oaks, but not the other eleven acres comprising his mother's estate. That acerage he intended to keep and subdivide into residential lots.

Following a court controversy, the Salvation Army accepted Sidley's terms and took possession of The Oaks, minus the eleven acres. Shortly thereafter, Sidley bought the mansion back, the Salvation Army meanwhile using the money from the sale to pay off its mortgage on its headquarters and a temple in Racine. Earlier his mother, Mabelle

(Horlick) Sidley, had encountered difficulties over her attempt to give money to the Salvation Army. Whatever the outcome of that problem, the Salvation Army at its Temple, located at 1901 Washington Avenue, Racine, held a dedication ceremony in honor of Mabelle (Horlick) Sidley. The plaque unveiled at that ceremony held on April 16, 1942, recognized Mrs. Sidley as:

> *A staunch supporter of the Salvation Army whose beneficence has helped largely to make possible this temple of worship and service.*

> *Deceased:*

> *July Sixth, 1938*

The program included remarks made "In Memoriam" by Mabelle (Horlick) Sidley's brother, Alexander James (A.J.) Horlick, the last member of her immediate family to survive her.

William Horlick Sidley occupied The Oaks for a brief while following his rejection from the army for defective eyesight. In August of 1942, demolition of The Oaks began. It was carried out by Anthony Kratochv whose workers noted that the soundness and quality of the structure made it hard to destroy. Whatever could be salvaged was offered for sale. Sadly, the walnut panelling from the library was destroyed when the garage where it was being stored was burned to the ground. Furnishings, books, silver, and decorative items were taken to Milwaukee and sold. A newspaper account describing The Oaks and its demolition began with this:

> *It marked the passing of a red plush, gold-plated era in Racine's social life—a period of lavish entertainment and rich living—when a crew of workmen began to raze a many gabled Victorian mansion on Washington Avenue.*

Mabelle's brother, A.J., and A.J.'s wife, Bertha, maintained a much lower social profile than did the Sidleys. On February 16, 1898, Bertha had married A.J. in a private ceremony at the home of her father, Ernest Hueffner, who was a prominent local banker. Unlike the Sidleys,

"Alexander James (A.J,) and Bertha (Hueffner) Horlick
courtesy Racine Heritage Museum

who spent the first year of their marriage abroad, A.J. and Bertha honeymooned only briefly in America before Mr. Horlick returned to work at the family business in Racine.

A.J. Horlick began his education at public schools in his hometown before enrolling at Racine College, from which he graduated in 1893. In order to better learn about the Horlick company, A.J. performed all sorts of jobs there. Eventually his contacts with those in the pharmaceutical and medical professions led to his support of such groups as the Institute of the History of Pharmacy and the American Foundation for Pharmaceutical Education. And while never having attended there, at the age of 37 he was appointed to the University of Wisconsin Board of Regents, a position he had not even applied for.

Following the death of their oldest child, Alice Priscilla, A.J.'s parents, William and Arabella Horlick, had donated the Alice Horlick Hospital and the Alice Horlick Memorial Maternity Wing to St. Luke's Hospital. For 40 years A.J. Horlick remained active in hospital affairs, both as a board member and as a generous contributor. St. Luke's Hospital had been established in Racine by St. Luke's Episcopal Church, another on-going beneficiary of the Horlick family.

A.J. Horlick shared in his father's desire to recognize and remember veterans of the wars. As mayor of Racine from 1907 to 1911, it was A.J. Horlick who oversaw the creation of the Spanish American War Monument. Its dedication took place in Mound Cemetery on Memorial Day, 1909. At the city's other public cemetery, Graceland, William Horlick, Sr. provided for a Veteran's Post 76 burial plot along with a monument to the soldiers of World War I. And while neither William, Sr. nor A.J. Horlick ever owned an airplane, each of them contributed in their individual ways to the cause of aviation. In 1941, Horlick Air Field was opened (now renamed Batten Air Field). Almost half of the 267 acres it occupied had been owned by the Horlick estate and on many weekday noons, A.J. Horlick could be spotted eating his meal at the airport lunch counter.

According to those who knew him, A.J. Horlick was rather quiet and unassuming. As mayor he had revived the English custom of carolers singing on their neighbors' porches to awaken them on Christmas morning. He himself sang in the St. Luke's Episcopal Church choir and reportedly contributed 60 percent of the church organist's salary. Ever a lover of practical jokes, A.J. and his friend, George Rickeman, a local grocery store owner, decided one 4th of July to try out a scheme they had labored and laughed over. It involved filling the watering trough on Monument Square with liquid nitrogen, a form of dry ice. The idea was that when thirsty parade horses would come to the trough for a drink, their noses would bump against ice and not water. To their merriment and the astonishment of those watching, it worked.

A.J. was especially fond of children, including his own two daughters, Jeanette and Helen. A tale was told that one day a young factory worker was called to Mr. Horlick's office where he found A.J. waiting with a set of marbles. "Teach me to play so I can play with the children" was the request Horlick made of his employee. True or not, it remains a good story.

Remembered by his godson as "jovial and rotund and smelling of Turkish cigarettes," which he was fond of smoking, A.J. would hold the growing child on his knee whenever they came together for a visit. As his godson neared the age of 12, A.J. found himself ending the practice, explaining gently to the boy that he had grown too big to continue being held.

The Horlicks lived with their daughters in a large frame house on the corner of 10th and Main Streets, several blocks from where Bertha (Hueffner) Horlick had grown up on College Avenue. Bertha (Hueffner) Horlick was one of the first in Racine to own and operate a Detroit electric car. In appearance the vehicle was much like its gasoline counterpart, driven by the Horlicks' chauffeur, John, who rode a bicycle back and forth between home and work.

When it was time for the Horlick daughters, Jeanette and Helen, to marry, rounds of social gatherings were set into motion. Jeanette Horlick's engagement to Zalmon G. Simmons brought together two locally prominent families, the Simmons being owners of the Simmons Mattress Company in Kenosha. Prior to a wedding for 600 held at St. Luke's Episcopal Church, the couple was entertained at a bridal dinner given by the bride's aunt Mabelle (Horlick) Sidley at her lavish estate, The Oaks.

Shortly thereafter, Helen Horlick wed stockbroker Harold Sherman Bond of New York. That union took place at St. Chrysostom's Episcopal Church in Chicago with both the rehearsal dinner and the reception held in the Crystal Room of the Blackstone Hotel. The Bonds had one adopted son, James Horlick Bond. Jeanette (Horlick) Simmons and her husband divorced, following the birth of their two daughters, Patricia and Jeanette Simmons. Her second marriage was to John F. Bowles, Jr.

Like his father, William, Sr. and his brother, A.J., William Horlick, Jr. was described as a shy, retiring, self-effacing individual who enjoyed bringing pleasure and happiness to others. His "thoughtful inquiries on how to be of assistance to those in need and his prompt courteous written replies on matters brought to his attention" were qualities appreciated

65

by friends and associates alike. William, Jr. was especially close to and protective of his only surviving sister, Mabelle, his sister, Alice, having died when he was five.

William, Jr. was two years old when his parents moved back to Racine from Chicago. As had his older brother, A.J., young William attended a public grammar school and then Racine College. He later completed an engineering course at King's College in London, followed by three years of travel in Europe and the Orient.

William, Jr. returned home to join the family business where he was put in charge of production. In 1921 he was made a vice president and later served as both treasurer and chairman of the board. Perhaps because of the long hours he spent working, William Horlick's office was described as being more like a home than a place of business. Included in the office furnishings was a glass case holding an Egyptian mummy, brought back by Horlick from Egypt in 1902. Following his death, brother A.J. donated William's mummy, affectionately known as "Maltie," to the county museum where it remains on display as part of a Horlick exhibit. An engineering background no doubt aided in William, Jr.'s acquisition of four trademarks and seven patents. One of those patents was for can closure and sealing which were, without doubt, useful at the Horlick plant in Wisconsin.

As a bachelor with no children of his own, William Horlick, Jr. nonetheless took an active interest in the lives and welfare of young people, often providing the necessary funds for their schooling. But as with his father, many of the charitable contributions made by William, Jr. to educational projects were never made public. He was known, however, for his generous gifts of malted milk products to the needy and to the poor.

The financing and construction of Memorial Hall, dedicated to war veterans of Racine, were presided over by William Horlick, Jr. who served as president of the Memorial Hall Commission. During World War I he acted as treasurer for the local council of defense. An honorary member of the GAR (Grand Army of the Republic), Mr. Horlick was also a 32nd degree Mason, a drum major for the Tripoli Temple Band, an honorary member of the Milwaukee Police Band, and a curator (honorary member) of the Wisconsin State Historical Society.

According to a *Milwaukee Journal* article from 1929, William Horlick, Jr. had purchased for preservation the room in which Abraham Lincoln had slept at Abner Kirby's hotel in Milwaukee. Following its restoration, the room was presented by Horlick to Dr. W.E. Barton for his Foxboro, Massachusetts, Lincoln Museum. Internet records indicate that this museum no longer exists.

Along with the rest of his family, William Horlick, Jr. was a strong supporter of St. Luke's Hospital as well as a devoted member of St. Luke's Episcopal Church where one of his close friends, Dr. John G. Meachem III served as choir director. Three generations of doctors, the Meachems were, like the Horlicks, loyal Episcopalians. In his will, Dr. Meachem, Jr. had ordered that the family home at 905 Main Street be sold and the proceeds donated to St. Luke's Church. Following Dr.

William Horlick, Jr. and Dr. John G. Meachem III
courtesy Racine Heritage Museum

John Meachem, Jr.'s death, William Horlick, Jr. purchased the Meachem house and then gave it to the church to sell again, allowing the parish to realize twice the amount of the original Meachem bequest.

On December 2, 1902, William Horlick, Jr., along with fellow Horlick employees Edward Paul Kastler, Allen Harvey Barnes, and a fourth party, cousin Clarence Clausen Horlick, filed articles of organization with the state of Wisconsin for the purpose of forming Horlick's Athletic Association. Twenty $50 shares of stock made up the $1,000 total held by three of the four founders.

The stated purpose of the association was:

to engage in conduct and promote all kinds of games and athletic sports both those played indoors and outdoors and more particularly to engage in conduct and manage clubs and teams to play baseball, polo, cricket and other kinds of athletics and to manage teams and clubs to play whist, and to conduct a band, a gun club, and other like business and games...

Apparently their efforts paid off, for just two years later, in 1904, the Horlicks of Racine were named National Whist Champions and winners of the Hamilton Trophy.

William Horlick, Jr.'s love of sports and participation in them began when he was a child. If the Horlick children's chores were done by Saturday afternoon, they were allowed to play baseball. Recalled William, Jr.:

I remember making the uniforms for one of the Horlick baseball teams. I say I made them, but I actually bought overalls and cut off the legs and sewed up a hem and sewed stripes down the legs. I used mother's sewing machine. I was about 15, I believe.

A sport that William Horlick, Jr. was especially fond of and took an active part in was roller polo, described as being like a combination of polo and hockey played on roller skates. Roller polo matches were first played in Racine at Lakeside Auditorium, Third and Lake Avenue, on a hardwood maple rink measuring 120 by 140 feet, before crowds of 3,000 enthusiastic fans. On December 13, 1919, Lakeside Auditorium was destroyed by fire but not before Racine's Horlick team had triumphed. In 1904-1905 they were named Champions of Wisconsin. Their second rush that year was a teenager named Fritz Reichert who became known as the "Babe Ruth of roller polo" and was listed among the nation's greatest players. Reichert would reintroduce the sport during the Great Depression and become a national star once again from 1934 to 1936 at a time when it was said that the game's popularity found "one half of Racine on wheels."

It is interesting to note that while the Horlicks of Racine were promoting roller polo, some of their family members in England were engaged in the more traditional form of the sport, played on horseback. William, Jr.'s cousin Ernest and his fellow Cowley Manor teammates, including the Marquess of Blandford, defeated the team from Dunstall Hall during a match held in 1922. Ernest's brother, James, meanwhile, made yearly visits to the Racine family operation, beginning in 1920 and continuing through 1939. While we will never know, one wonders if James ever accompanied William, Jr. to a roller polo match, so beloved by the American cousin who proudly played on the Horlick team.

Margo Drummond

VI. THEIR SEPARATE WAYS

On Saturday, May 7, 1921, it was announced that Sir James Horlick had died at his London residence, Number Two Carlton House Terrace. He was seventy-seven years old. Funeral services were held at the chapel near his Cowley Manor estate in Gloucestershire, where Sir James was to be buried.

The death of Sir James created enormous tax, financial and family problems which appeared to be best resolved by splitting into two parts the company that he and his brother, William, had founded. A logical way to do so was to give William the American business covering North and South America and the Caribbean. Sir James' sons, Ernest and James, would take over the English company covering Europe, Asia, Africa and Australia. Each entity would operate separately while maintaining contact with one another for the exchange of information. In 1926 arrangements were completed and the breakup took place.

Horlick Production—Slough, England
courtesy Horlick Museum, Slough, England

During the early 1900's, prior to World War I, it was commonplace in Racine for men of wealth and prominence to serve in public office and, if not to compete, at least to match one another in generous gifts bestowed upon their fellow citizens. There clearly was a spirit of what might be termed benevolent paternalism within the community during those years. Factory owners and factory workers hunted, fished and picnicked together, often in parks named Horlick or Johnson.

William Horlick had begun the process by donating 20 acres of land to the city for Horlick and Island Parks. The renowned landscape architect, Jens Jensen, was chosen to do the designs. School board member, H.F. Johnson, grandson of S.C. Johnson, who had founded S.C. Johnson Wax Company, and William Horlick together helped to secure the land for two of the city's public high schools. Sometime later, H.F. Johnson's son, Sam, would tell about going to his father with the news that he had found a better summer job than his dad could offer him. It seemed that Horlick's was offering $50 a week, twice what young Sam could make working for his father at S.C. Johnson's. Recalled Sam Johnson of the incident, "My pay got much better the year after that."

And while Horlick's was never renowned for offering its workers high wages (seven cents an hour being the starting salary in 1911), the company did offer them something else. When the number of employees at the Horlick plant in Racine reached several hundred, William Horlick formed a Horlick cricket team which he played on himself, as he once had while a boy growing up in England. He also introduced the Saturday half holiday. According to his son, A.J., William Horlick was the first businessman in America to try the five and a half day work week for factory workers. Added brother, William, Jr., "Father knew every man who worked in the plant by his first name, and he got more genuine pleasure out of playing cricket and later baseball with his employees than in any other activity."

William Horlick had hired many of his employees personally. Known to them as "Mr. Bill," he was said to have been crushed when, in 1934, there was a strike at the plant in Racine. What got him through the personal hurt of the incident was the knowledge that those who went on strike were not his longtime loyal employees but rather a group more recently hired, and not by him. It was not the strike, however, but other factors that adversely affected the fortunes of Horlick's in America following World War I. A marketing study done for the company in 1946 cites several reasons for the decline in sales of Horlick's products distributed from Wisconsin beginning in 1921 when sales dropped over 15 percent. Many of the reasons could be directly attributed to the changes in American lifestyle following the war.

Prior to the war drugstores were perceived as just that, places to purchase medicines and prescribed remedies. Druggists were trusted by their patrons to dispense advice on all sorts of health-related issues including nutritional ones. Understanding that well-intentioned druggist-patron relationship, the Horlick's marketing department had shrewdly tapped into it by courting both pharmacists and drugstore owners. James Horlick had done it, so had his nephew, A.J., and as a consequence, Horlick's was routinely recommended as a panacea for all sorts of health-related problems.

Likewise, pediatricians urged mothers of their infant patients to feed their babies Horlick's. That is, until after the war when several things changed. A growing middle class contributed to the education of more and better-trained doctors. As a result, the study of nutrition got a closer look and suddenly infant diets became infused with castor oil and orange juice and a variety of other foods which replaced Horlick's as the mainstay.

Another change in the sales of Horlick's resulted from the fact that, following the war, more and more people gained access to automobiles. Stores could be located further away from home which meant they could also be larger and contain more products. Both grocery and drugstores thus expanded their inventories to include a lot more than just drug or food items. For Horlick's that created a problem because, as retail had changed, so had the image of their malted milk product. No longer was it simply a health food but in the eyes of the younger generation it was now equated with confectionery items sold at soda fountains and known not as Horlick's but simply as malted milk.

Older users who went looking for Horlick's where they had always found it, at the drugstore, were confused to learn that malted milk was no longer handled by the druggist, but rather along with a burgeoning array of processed foods, on the shelves of grocery stores. Meanwhile, at the increasingly popular soda fountains of America, consumption habits were also changing. Coca-Cola was fast becoming the drink of choice for those seeking "the pause that refreshes." Flat-chested flappers in particular preferred it to calorie-laden malts that threatened to fill out their slim-hipped figures.

And, whereas before the war Horlick's had had a seeming monopoly on the malted milk market, the rise of Bordens, Carnation, Ovaltine and others who had been able to duplicate the formula, just as James Horlick had feared, made competition a reality that Horlick's struggled to deal with. Their answer was to separate the original dietary food from the soda fountain confection. This they did by setting up a subsidiary company, the Milkos Food Company, to sell their confectionery product. When it became clear that such a diversionary tactic was not succeeding, the Horlick's Fountain Brand took the place of Milkos. But, unfortunately much of the damage had already been done.

More and more people in America came to equate Horlick's with the sweet soda fountain confectionery creations believed to have originated with a Mississippi drug store owner who substituted the powder for milk one day, rather than with the dietary product once recommended by their local druggists. Beginning in 1925, sales took a precipitous dive that culminated in 1932 sales falling below those for 1899. An exhaustive advertising campaign lessened the decline but at a tremendous cost. By 1937, over 45 percent of every dollar earned was being spent on marketing the Horlick name.

It was during the early 1930's that William Horlick signed a contract with radio personalities Lum and Abner to sponsor their show. As a token of gratitude, the pair presented Mr. Horlick with a black cocker spaniel puppy named The Duke of Pine Ridge, Pine Ridge being the name of their radio program. The dog, featured in many photographs with his master, clearly offered comfort and companionship to an aging

William Horlick as he faced the prospect of losing much of what he had spent his life creating.

Meanwhile, thanks in large part to brother James, a clear and solid market for Horlick's had been established in England, Europe, and most of the British Empire. In a piece he wrote entitled, "A Brief History of Horlick's," a longtime company employee, Patrick Campbell, made some interesting observations based on his work with both the British and later the American Horlick's. Referring to the division that had taken place in the company following the death of Sir James in 1921, he wrote:

> *As things turned out, this was probably just as well for the English company. Mr. William Horlick had become very rich, both from the business and judicious property investments. He still dominated everything including his two sons, and methods of Racine had not changed much with the times, all of which hampered marketing progress and decision making as far as the English business was concerned.*

Free from its American "cousin," a reorganized Horlick's Malted Milk (England) modernized and moved forward. With Ernest Horlick as chairman, James as head of sales, and cousin Oliver as managing director of production, a new management team and sales staff were put into place. To further insure success, a new advertising agency was employed, the highly regarded J. Walter Thompson firm. At the first meeting, Mr. Sam Mach of J. Walter Thompson was said to have asked, "Who buys malted milk and why?" to which he received the answer, "We're damned if we know."

With that the advertising firm introduced to Horlick's England a relatively new merchandising development known as market research which focused upon the public consumption of a product, its competitive situation, and the general reasons for which food drinks then on the British market were consumed. What resulted was a decision to create the image of a product with specific rather than general appeal. Known simply as "Horlick's," that product shed the commodity image associated with malted milk that so plagued Horlick's Malted Milk in America as it became too closely identified with the soda fountain trade. The new Horlick's was advocated as a purveyor of a sound night's sleep, if taken before bedtime, as illustrated in the Night Starvation Story cartoons. Internationally the "night starvation" concept became known as FAJA KI KAMZORI in India, meaning "weakness of the early morning." To the Chinese it meant, "If your spirit is weak in the morning." It was likewise touted as the perfect mid-morning or afternoon beverage for school children. Such global successes kept Horlick's England sales growing steadily until the onset of World War II in 1938.

During World War II, Horlick's Malted Milk products were used as part of the rations sent along with the troops overseas. A *Racine Journal Times* article dated January 26, 1942, reported that 150 million malted milk tablets were being delivered to U.S. armed forces. Easy to carry and at just six calories each, Horlick's Malted Milk tablets provided sustenance for all branches of the military including balloonists and bombing crews as well as for those aboard life rafts and barges.

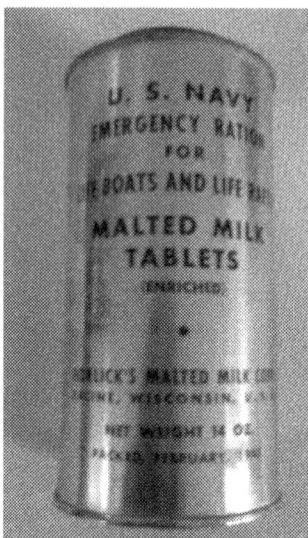

Horlick Malted Milk Tablet Rations—World War II
courtesy Jim Mercier, photo by Judy Moungey

An August 2, 1942, *New York Times* story described how a group of survivors, burned when their oil tanker was attacked by the Germans, talked of food as they clung to their life boat. A juicy tenderloin smothered in onions or chicken and gravy was what one man dreamed of. "Will you settle for a malted milk tablet and canteen water instead?" he was asked. "Sure," was the answer reported by Ensign Lewis John Muevy, Jr., U.S.N.R., who survived the ordeal, having been rescued later on.

About a month later three naval crewmen had their boat overturned during a South Pacific squall. Subsequently the boat was bumped on the bottom by sharks, causing all their food supplies to be lost. After 23 days the three were rescued, having subsisted on three bottles of Horlick's tablets.

In October of that same year, Captain Edward (Eddie) Rickenbacker, the celebrated flying ace, was forced, along with his crew, to abandon his plane. Rickenbacker and three of the crew floated on a life raft in the South Pacific for 24 days, during which time one of the crew members died and was buried at sea. Until their rescue, Rickenbacker and the others survived on K-rations which included biscuits, canned meat, chewing gum and Horlick's malted milk tablets.

On another raft were fellow crew members, Lt. James C. Whittaker, along with Lt. John J. de Angelis and Staff Sergeant James Reynolds. By the end of their ordeal only Lt. Whittaker, known as "the strong man," had energy enough to keep rowing their raft. "One of the craziest things that developed," Whittaker later told reporters, "was a craving for strawberry malted milk shakes." Nearly every day the men would talk back and forth saying, "How about fixing me a strawberry malted milk shake?"

When they finally beached on an island, instead of malted milk shakes they found only coconuts, mackerel, and uncooked rats for food. "The rats weren't bad," commented Whittaker, "but you had to be pretty hungry to eat them." Except for Alexander Kaczmarezyk, who perished, all members of the Rickenbacker crew were eventually accounted for, including the pilot of the plane, William Chevy.

Upon his return home, Lt. Whittaker headed for a soda fountain where he hoped to satisfy his craving for a strawberry malted milk shake. To his dismay, the soda fountain was out of malted milk, due to the high demand for it by the military. Captain Rickenbacker had better luck. Taken to Hawaii, Rickenbacker requested ten malted milk shakes, all of which were brought to him. As he recalled it, he could only finish one.

Following the Rickenbacker rescue, Horlick's Malted Milk Corporation was declared, "an essential and vital industry." But by February of 1944, as the war entered its final phases, the War Food Administration issued an order rationing the sale and control of the production of dried milk powder. A year later, in 1945, the English and American companies were reunited and with that, further changes begun by war were set into motion.

VII. THINGS CHANGE

Family-owned companies, when placed in the hands of outside management, understandably experience change. So it was with Horlick's, having been purchased in 1945 by its English counterpart. One longtime Racine Horlick employee described how in the fall of 1945, three executives and a secretary arrived from England to "make a survey of our operations." In later years, that same gentleman told of how he worked in advertising, "but with English standards."

It was not the difference in management style so much as the transitory nature of operations that seemed to be felt by those who had known Horlick's as a locally owned and operated concern. As corporate structures and personnel were shuffled and reshuffled, the so-called "outsiders" who came and went with such reorganization had no particular interest in the place where they lived, other than that they worked there. Such simple things as the 4th of July Parade, traditionally enhanced by employee-made floats and company marching bands became suddenly "less local."

"Horlick Employee's Parade—Racine, Wisconsin (circa World War I)
courtesy Racine Heritage Museum

There is a classic photograph, taken in 1909, of Mayor A.J. Horlick, along with six other former mayors of Racine, seated in an open automobile. The occasion was a (so-called) "homecoming parade." Names familiar to local Racine residents included Mayor M.M. Secor, a Bohemian trunk manufacturer, Frank Mitchell of the Mitchell Lewis Motor Company, David G. Janes, a descendant of some of the city's earliest settlers, and Ernest Hueffner, A.J. Horlick's father-in-law. But as has so often been the case, industries and enterprises passed on to second and third generations frequently do not remain in family hands. Such was the fate of many of Racine's 100 locally owned operations, sadly including Horlick's Malted Milk.

Along with the influences of two world wars on the fortunes of Horlick's in America, family problems were also to blame. At the close of his will, written some years before his death in 1936 at the age of 90, William Horlick had chastened his three children to remember the following:

> *The success of the business of manufacturing Horlick's Malted Milk was because I practiced industry, intelligence, and frugality. I caution my sons and daughter in causing the business to be continued and in its management and in their own private affairs to practice industry, intelligence, frugality and cooperation.*

Those words would prove to be both prophetic and haunting.

While sailing to England, William Horlick, Jr. had met and befriended a British barrister, W. Perkins Bull, K.C. (King's Counselor). The meeting occurred, coincidentally, because both Bull and Horlick had neatly-trimmed beards causing fellow passengers to mistake them for one another. After several such incidents, W. Perkins Bull approached William Horlick, Jr. and having looked him over, said, "Oh now I see why people keep calling me Mr. Horlick. You must be Mr. Horlick."

Their friendship established, it was further strengthened by another case of mistaken identity as they departed the ship. The chauffeur of a waiting limousine with the royal coat-of-arms hailed William

Horlick, thinking that he was Mr. Bull. Amused by the mix-up, Horlick played along, letting the chauffeur take his luggage. Not far behind, W. Perkins Bull came to the red-faced driver's rescue. To Horlick he said, "I was going to invite you to ride with me anyway."

Bull, who owned estates in Canada, Cuba and China, was said to be a frequent guest at Windsor Castle. According to London gossip sheets, when Mr. Bull and King George played billiards, it was "Right-o, Willie," and "Well played, George." William Horlick, Jr., who had reportedly entertained Edward VII, Prince of Wales, in both Racine and Chicago on occasion, did not hesitate to ask Bull to be his guest following their trans-Atlantic crossing. Bull accepted the invitation, paying a visit to Racine in 1927 at which time he was introduced to Horlick's sister, Mabelle (Horlick) Sidley during a gathering at her estate, The Oaks. According to Mrs. Sidley's personal maid, Mae Harrison, from that point on, W. Perkins Bull "became the life of the house at The Oaks, practically running it." He also quickly became Mrs. Sidley's personal lawyer.

Two years later, in 1929, Mabelle (Horlick) Sidley sued her husband for divorce on the grounds of desertion. At the time Dr. Sidley's brother, William, was president of the Chicago Bar Association as well as a member of one of Chicago's most prestigious law firms. A lawsuit brought by Dr. John Sidley in June of 1931 asked for $250,000 in damages against W. Perkins Bull. According to Sidley's attorney, Bull had had Sidley shadowed by private detectives for three years, resulting in both physical and psychological damage to Dr. Sidley's health. Named as a co-defendant in the suit was J.J. Harrison, head of the detective agency allegedly used by Bull and more interestingly, the former husband of Mabelle (Horlick) Sidley's personal maid, Mae.

At the time of his parents' separation, William Horlick Sidley, then 18, had chosen to live with his father who had taken up residence at The Elms Apartments in Racine. One reason for having detectives follow John Sidley and his son may have had to do with Mrs. Sidley's desire to obtain custody of her only child. Perhaps she was hoping that she could get something to use against her husband in that effort.

81

For a family as prominent and as private as the Horlicks, such publicity had to have been more than distressful. According to those who knew them, it was William Horlick, Jr. who sided with his sister and his parents against brother A.J. who had warned each of his family members to beware of W. Perkins Bull. Shortly before the Sidley divorce became final, Dr. Sidley dropped his lawsuit against W. Perkins Bull, K.C. That must have come as a great relief to the Horlicks who had dreaded the testimony Dr. Sidley had threatened to give regarding the relationship of his estranged wife and Mr. Bull.

Terms of the Sidley divorce, decreed on Saturday afternoon, February 21, 1931, in Kenosha, were kept sealed. Those in attendance at the proceedings were Mabelle (Horlick) Sidley, her father, William, and her brother, William, Jr. A.J. Horlick did not appear. It was rumored that Dr. John Streeter Sidley received a hefty settlement, by some estimates about $10,000 per year for his lifetime. Twelve months later John Sidley married Madelon Wilson, a California socialite. Dr. Sidley died in 1936 at the age of 57.

A point made repeatedly about the cause of the decline of Horlick's Racine had to do with a growing lack of interest in the product by the so-called "rising generation." A similar point might be made about the American branch of the Horlick family. There simply was no "rising generation" stepping forward with new ideas and fresh enthusiasm, once the hallmarks of the Horlick brothers, James and William.

Following their respective marriages, A.J.'s daughters, Jeanette and Helen, had moved to Greenwich, Connecticut. Their only cousin, William Horlick Sidley, was known in Racine as a "spoiled rich kid" who drove around town in a Dusenburg, displaying no interest whatsoever in joining the family business. His grandfather and namesake, William Horlick Sr., was fast approaching 90 and by some accounts could not let go of the entity he had so painstakingly created, leaving his sons, A.J. and William, Jr. to flounder. Not a lot is known about the role Arabella Horlick played during those years following the war, but as a mother she was no doubt conflicted over growing dissension among her children.

Unlike her daughter and granddaughters, Arabella Horlick's name did not appear in society columns describing lavish bridal showers, country club golf outings and costume balls, one of which found the rich dressed in garb imitating the poor. During the years when they still lived in Chicago, Arabella Horlick reportedly stayed up nights preparing batches of Horlick's on a basement stove. Later on, as a woman of enormous wealth, she still delighted in churning her own butter and making cottage cheese to be shared with friends. One indulgence she did allow herself was having silver buttons custom made for her clothing. Following their creation, she ordered that the molds be destroyed so that no one else would have buttons like hers.

Arabella Roselia (Horlick) Horlick
courtesy Racine Heritage Museum

83

Mrs. Horlick shared in her son William's talent for invention. The patent for a dough-raising cupboard was recorded and held in her name. She also shared a family tradition of keeping private one's philanthropic efforts. Numerous photographs of Arabella Horlick, including one with her husband and daughter following the dedication of a YMCA bus they had donated, could be found in local newspapers and magazines. She was frequently named as an honorary chairperson of some civic or charitable organization. But beyond that, who Arabella Roselia (Horlick) Horlick really was remains largely unknown.

Photographs taken of the Horlicks during the earlier years of their marriage would seem to reflect a close relationship shared by the couple. Someone who worked for them said that, as the years went on, however, they could be found seated at either end of a long dining room table, communicating not directly with one another any longer but through the butler. Mr. Horlick might instruct the butler to inform Mrs. Horlick that he was going to England for six weeks. Mrs. Horlick might then reply, once again via a servant. Whatever the truth of their relationship, the marriage endured for 65 years.

When William Horlick died of cerebral thrombosis at the age of 90 in 1936, he left behind an estate of some twenty to thirty million dollars. To his wife, Arabella, he left their home and all its furnishings, approximately one million dollars, and a $3,000 monthly allowance. By some accounts Mrs. Horlick had amassed a small fortune on her own, independent of her husband. Mr. Horlick named his three children, A.J., William, Jr. and Mabelle as co-executors and beneficiaries, to share equally in company stock and capital amounting to somewhere between five and seven million dollars each. It was left to the three of them to run their father's business. A.J. Horlick took over as president, William, Jr. became treasurer and chairman of the board, and Mabelle was appointed secretary. Still plagued by scandal, she had been living off and on at the home of W. Perkins Bull at Number 3, Meredith Crescent in Toronto, Canada, much to the dismay of her oldest brother, A.J.

Prior to her father's death, Mabelle had returned from Bull's home in Toronto to help care for him. Their mutual love of baseball and music had kept the two close, and it was Mabelle who would often sing for her father as he worked in his "office," which in later years was located in the Horlick home. The word William Horlick used to describe his daughter's singing was "relaxing." "When she played the piano and sang for me," he added, "it helped me concentrate on business." He credited her with knowing more about sports than almost anyone and often quipped that she could have been a worthy baseball team manager. Both father and daughter no doubt enjoyed the fact that at the 1920 Olympic Games, Horlick tablets were consumed by participating athletes.

In 1938, A.J. Horlick petitioned the courts to remove his sister as an executor of their father's will, based on questions of her mental competency. The petition was denied but there seemed to be cause for concern. Mabelle's personal fortune was rapidly dwindling and in her own will, written that year, she left a third of her estate to W. Perkins Bull, the will having been drafted by one of Bull's law partners.

Testimony given by Mae Harrison, Mabelle's personal maid and companion, described Mabelle (Horlick) Sidley as exhibiting signs of confusion, paranoia and exhaustion as she neared the end of her life. "Mrs. Sidley was often sent out for the day and evening on lengthy car rides by Mr. Bull," stated Mrs. Harrison. Despite the fact that she was in Toronto, Mrs. Sidley would sometimes ask the driver to drop her off at the Horlick's Malted Milk factory in Racine so that she could visit her mother. She would also approach strangers whom she fantasized were her son, reported Mrs. Harrison, who accompanied Mrs. Sidley on these car rides. Sometimes she requested that the stranger give her a kiss. All in all, Mabelle (Horlick) Sidley seemed to have drifted far from the images of her as a beautiful child with long dark hair who was seen galloping through the countryside on her pony, Black Beauty, or driving herself to school in a horse-drawn phaeton.

Mabelle (Horlick) Sidley died at the home of W. Perkins Bull in Toronto on July 6, 1938, at 6:15 in the morning. Questions about the cause of death (believed by her son, William Horlick Sidley, to have been caused by slow poisoning) would linger, but it was officially listed as a heart attack. Word of her daughter's death reached a frail Arabella

Horlick, herself bedridden and barely clinging to life. The funeral that was planned for Mabelle had to be postponed when it was learned that Arabella had died only three days after her youngest child. The date of Arabella Roselia (Horlick) Horlick's death, July 9, 1938, followed her 88th birthday. During her lifetime Mrs. Horlick had taken delight in observing the Australian swans who graced the pond created for them on the Horlick property. On the day she died, one of the swans was found dead as well. Was it mere coincidence or as some believed, more meaningful? We will never know.

July 9th, Arabella (Horlick) Horlick's death date, had also been the date chosen for daughter Mabelle's funeral. Instead of services at St. Luke's as first announced, private services were held for mother and daughter some days later at the Horlick home where both William and Arabella Horlick had died and where Mabelle Horlick had been born.

William Horlick, Jr. continued to live in his parents' home for another two years until on April 1, 1940, he died of complications resulting from a bout of influenza. At the time of his death, William Horlick, Jr. was 64 years old. Funeral services for William Horlick, Jr. were held at St. Luke's Episcopal Church, with Masonic rites performed at the family mausoleum.

Having suffered the loss of his father, his mother, his sister, and his brother within four years of one another, it was left to A.J. Horlick to manage the family business and residual legal affairs alone. He did so until 1945 when the American Horlick's was bought out by the British arm whose rise had paralleled its decline. Problems over the wording of his mother's will and taxes due on his father's vast estate had occupied much of A.J.'s time. In September of 1949 his beloved wife, Bertha, died. He survived her by only nine months.

A.J. Horlick's funeral service, like those of family members who preceded him in death, was held at St. Luke's Episcopal Church. Outside the church, a police escort kept Main Street free of traffic while waiting to accompany Mr. Horlick's remains to Mound Cemetery. Inside the church banked with red and white flowers, the choir that A.J. Horlick had been a part of sang his three favorite hymns, "Onward Christian Soldiers," "The Church's One Foundation," and "Abide With Me."

A tribute offered in A.J. Horlick's memory by the City Council of Racine could just as aptly have applied to his father, his brother, his uncle James, and his English cousins, each of whom had lived his life with the understanding that those to whom much is given, should give much in return. The tribute read:

> *Whereas, Alexander J. Horlick has both in his public and private life ever been conscious of the welfare of the people of this city:*
>
> *Whereas, during his entire lifetime Alexander Horlick has given unselfishly and unsparingly of his time and energy with no expectation of any return except the satisfaction arising from having contributed to the welfare of his community;*
>
> *Now, therefore, be it resolved by the Common Council of the City of Racine that we express our sincere regret at the death of Alexander J. Horlick who for so many years served as an outstanding mayor of the City of Racine, and that we tender our sympathy to his bereaved family.*

Within 20 years of A.J. Horlick's death, the company that he and his family had helped to create was bought out by the Beecham food and pharmaceutical conglomerate in England for twenty million pounds. Beecham would eventually become part of GlaxoSmithKline, which today produces forty-two million pounds of Horlick's per year and claims to have discovered the 130-year-old secret of why Horlick's sends people to sleep—it's something to do with its iron and vitamin content. Horlick's is now being marketed as a daytime reliever of stress and a nighttime aid to a more restful sleep.

At a factory built in Punjab, India, in 1960, Horlick's began producing their product with the use of buffalo milk. Horlick production plants in

West Punjab, Pakistan, and Bangladesh soon followed. From 1975-1978, factory construction and expansion were completed in Andhra, Pradesh. Horlick's also established a hold in Australia and New Zealand, as well as in the Philippines, where they sold milky-chocolate-flavored disks to be eaten like candy.

Meanwhile, by 1975, the greatly reduced Racine operation of Horlick's was ended altogether. Those castle-like buildings designed by William Horlick became occupied by various other industries and interests. Today, still structurally sound, they await reinvention through alternative uses. Sadly, they remain one of the few tangible reminders of a rich and vibrant era once fostered and sustained in large part by the Horlicks of Racine.

VIII. "MR. BILL"

I will try this day to live a simple, sincere and serene life, expelling every thought of discontent, self-seeking and anxiety; cultivate magnanimity, self-control and the habit of silence, practicing economy, cheerfulness and helpfulness. And as I cannot on my own strength do this or even with the hope of success attempt it, I look to Thee O Lord, my Father in Jesus Christ, my Savior and ask for the gift of the Holy Spirit.

That was the prayer that William Horlick kept on his desk and the one he recited at the beginning of each business day. A devout Episcopalian, Mr. Horlick practiced his beliefs both in the conduct of his personal life as well as in public affairs, perhaps explaining why to friends and fellow workers alike he was often affectionately referred to as, "Mr. Bill."

During the early 1920's the Horlick plant in Racine employed about a thousand workers. It was customary for William Horlick to make daily visits to the 500,000 square-foot facility, at that time one of the largest in America. It was also customary that Horlick workers be served malted milk each morning and afternoon. As the story goes, on one such walk-through, Mr. Horlick approached an employee and inquired of him, "Well, Pat, have you had a drink today?" "Oh no, Mr. Horlick," was the quick reply, "not one drop have I had since last night." "I meant malted milk," responded the bemused manufacturer. "Thank you kindly, sir," offered back his employee, adding, "but I will if you haven't something a wee bit stronger."

On each floor of his Racine factory, William Horlick had included enormous walk-in safes complete with ventilation to keep the cash used to pay the workers' salaries from getting musty. At the time of his death, Horlick's personal fortune, much of it in cash, was estimated to be between twenty and thirty million dollars. Of that, he left to anyone in his employ for twenty years or more a full year's salary with special

89

gifts of $5,000 to personal assistants and $10,000 to his secretary of 45 years, Andrea Pultz. Also named as beneficiaries were numerous relatives including nieces, nephews, and cousins.

Two statements regarding money were attributed to William Horlick. "It's too bad," he reflected, "that people only think about money, too bad," adding, "It's not money that's important, what's important is saving lives." Having experienced the death of several siblings as well as that of his oldest child, Alice Priscilla, William Horlick directed his adult energies to saving the lives of not only infants and invalids who benefited from the Horlick formula, but those disadvantaged children in his local community as well. Children of parents who could not afford to pay a doctor's fee were nonetheless treated by physicians sworn to secrecy over who had sent them. Oftentimes it was Mr. Horlick himself who sat up nights at the bedside of a sick or dying child. His own sons, A.J. and William, Jr., were cautioned by their father not to speak of these missions.

But some years after his father died, William Horlick, Jr. did recall that for two nights in a row Horlick Sr. had been mysteriously "missing." Questioned by his sons as to his whereabouts, Mr. Horlick explained that he had been at the bedside of a dying child. As the child's distraught mother stood by, physicians called in by Horlick explained to her and to him that there was no hope of saving the baby from pneumonia. At that point William Horlick took over, spoon feeding his formula to the infant, drop by drop. "By some miracle," as the doctors later described it, Mr. Horlick nursed the child back to health. "I would like to know," mused William Horlick, Jr. in recounting the story, "whatever happened to that baby."

When the eleven-year old son of Horlick's chauffeur was accidentally scalded by water that had been boiling on the stove, it was likely that William Horlick once again called in his team of doctors. Sadly, no one was able to save the boy's life. Sad too for William Horlick who counted his driver, Benjamin Olson, as both a friend and frequent fishing partner. Surely the tragedy must have reminded him of when his own child, Alice Priscilla, had died at that very same age.

On the afternoon of February 10, 1882, Alice's father had taken her to Harbridge's Store in downtown Racine. From there she proceeded to the Home School for a music lesson, after which she joined some of her friends in play. It was at that point that Alice Horlick collapsed into convulsions. Carried upstairs, she was watched over by a Mrs. McMurphy until Dr. Meachem arrived. Young Alice never regained consciousness, and, at five o'clock, following further convulsions, she died.

Funeral services for Alice Priscilla Horlick were held at St. Stephen's Episcopal Church on Northwestern Avenue, not far from her parents' home. In her memory, a baptismal font was given to the church. It is now at St. Nicholas Episcopal Church in West Racine, St. Stephen's having been disbanded. Both the Alice Horlick Maternity Hospital and the Alice Horlick Memorial Hospital, two segments of St. Luke's Hospital, were given to the community by members of the Horlick family, each of whom continued to share both money and their time in support of those medical facilities for the remainder of their lives.

Long before his own death, William Horlick's gift giving had become legendary. His generous offerings to explorers such as Admiral Richard Byrd, including funding for a Curtiss Condor aircraft which Byrd named the "William Horlick," prompted Byrd to dub a range of hills on the edge of the Transantartic Ross Ice Shelf in Antarctica the

"The William Horlick" Curtiss Condor
courtesy Racine Heritage Museum

91

Horlick Mountains. Another was named for Horlick's daughter, Mabelle (Horlick) Sidley. An elderly Mr. Horlick can be seen in a photograph, standing beside crates of his malted milk product that would accompany Admiral Byrd on his Antarctic expedition.

Ever excited over the prospects of discovery brought forth by world exploration, William Horlick would no doubt have loved the fact that his malted milk tablets eventually reached the moon, taken there by the astronauts who first set foot on it. Mr. Horlick had religiously followed the Byrd expedition by radio upon his return home from New York where he had seen Byrd off. According to those with him at the time, it was almost as though he himself had led the venture, so intense was his absorption of it.

William Horlick's passion for exploration was rivaled by another, that for sports. On September 4, 1935, he attended the dedication of the Horlick Athletic Field, given as a gift to the citizens of Racine by him and his family. A photograph taken that day shows a bespectacled William Horlick with his signature bow tie, boutonniere, and neatly-trimmed beard. In that photo he is wearing a three-piece suit as he often did for another favorite activity, that of fishing. Alongside him in the photograph is a man identified as the governor, and a woman who would appear to be Horlick's daughter, Mabelle, although because she was not facing the camera at the time, it is impossible to tell for certain. Whomever the lady pictured might be, her hat and gloves and the fur piece draped over one shoulder attest to a lifestyle long gone.

During World War II, Mr. Horlick's athletic field would become home to the Racine Belles, featured in the movie, "A League Of Their Own." Both the Belles and their female opponents were required to play women's baseball in short skirts, a tradition that ended, like so many, as things changed following the end of the war. One thing that did not change was the Horlick name affixed to the five-acre complex. That it always remain Horlick Athletic Field was part of the agreement made between the Horlicks and Racine, a city once known as the "belle" or beautiful city of the Great Lakes. The only other stipulation made by the family was that the site not be made a park. Having given both

Horlick and Island Parks to the city early on, the field was designated "to promote interest in athletics, sports activities, military drills, musical events and amusements," instead. Himself an expert on cricket and other sports as well as a great lover of music, William Horlick made sure that his beloved community would have access to both during events held at Horlick Field, which they do to this day.

Worldly and affluent as he was, William Horlick never allowed himself to forget his humble beginnings. As a reminder, he kept a battered coronet that he had played while still a youth in England. Another prized possession from the past was his set of saddle-making tools. They were among the first things listed in his will, a gift to his son, William, Jr. Other personal items, which included portraits of his parents and a few of his mother's dishes, went to A.J. and Mabelle, the bequest to each child totaling approximately $50. Later on in the will, about $5 million was bequeathed to each of the three surviving Horlick siblings by their father. Yet it was clear the mementos of his past rather than the fortune he had accumulated during his lifetime were what William Horlick considered of ultimate value, given their prominence and detailed descriptions at the outset of his thirty-six-page will.

In later years it was said of Mr. Horlick that he might spend half a day selecting the finest leather for his boots and shoes. But he also took time to make for his son, A.J., a saddle much like the one he had reportedly crafted for one of President Grant's brothers, when he first arrived in Chicago from England. A local Racine resident recalled how her father would set aside the best apples from his orchard each fall for Mr. Horlick's personal selection and purchase. Having spent his childhood among the orchards of Ruardean, he never lost his appreciation for such things. Not only did simple pleasures remain a part of William Horlick's life, but his desire and willingness to share them with others remained as well. He was equally comfortable and at home fishing along the Root River in Racine with his friend and employee, Benjamin Olson, as he was fishing with neighbors of his at his Millionaire's Row mansion in Florida or at his lodge in Moose Jaw, Saskatchewan.

Driving himself in an electric buggy, Mr. Horlick often made the short trip between his office and a local restaurant, Little Bohemia, on Douglas Avenue. One year just before Christmas he brought along a fruit cake for Mrs. Altman who worked there. Upon hearing of the gift, three other female employees of the restaurant including Mrs. Altman's niece, Virginia, expressed their wish to Mr. Horlick that they be given fruit cakes as well. In exchange for the fruit cakes they promised him a "kiss." Several days later the cakes they had requested arrived, prompting the three of them to fashion a corsage out of Hershey kisses which they mailed to Mr. Horlick. According to Mrs. Altman, he was "thrilled at their cleverness."

It was not surprising that some 3,600 people came to pay their respects to Mr. Horlick following his death, many of them on foot or by bicycle. The funeral and burial services which followed reflected the deep esteem and profound affection felt for "Mr. Bill" by so many who inhabited the community he had loved and shared in. Following private services for family and close friends held at home, William Horlick's remains were removed to St. Luke's Episcopal Church where his casket lay surrounded by floral tributes from 21 foreign countries. For their personal tribute the family chose a blanket of dwarf white chrysanthemums and daisies, reflecting the simplicity William Horlick had cherished and maintained throughout his lifetime.

Twelve hundred people attended the funeral service which was performed by Bishop Harwood Sturtevant of Fond du Lac and Reverend Henry Roth, dean of Milwaukee's All Saints Cathedral, two long-time family friends. The St. Luke's Boys' Choir sang Mr. Horlick's three favorite hymns, "Lead Kindly Light," "The Church's One Foundation," and "Abide With Me," while numerous Horlick employees, seated in a special section of the sanctuary, looked on. Several Horlick employees also served as pallbearers. Among them were L.H. Nickelson, executive secretary, E.P. Kastler, advertising manager, Edward Bolbeck, foreman, and department heads A.H. Barnes, W.D. Thomas, and D.H. Casterton. They were joined by Mr. Horlick's grandson, William Horlick Sidley, and his personal physician, Dr. Eric Von Buddenbock. In accordance with William Horlick's will, each pallbearer was provided with a pair of white kidskin gloves for the occasion.

Included in the funeral procession were many of the civic and community groups that Mr. Horlick and his family had supported. Spanish American War Veterans, in whose honor son, A.J. Horlick, had secured a monument at Mound Cemetery, marched to the church from Memorial Hall. The creation of Memorial Hall to honor war veterans had been overseen by William Horlick, Jr. At the entrance to Mound Cemetery stood lines of Boy Scouts, paying tribute to Mr. Horlick who had once served as honorary chairman of their organization. Alongside the burial vault were sixteen American Legion drum and bugle corps members. Horlick Field regularly played host to drum and bugle corps events, Racine being known as the Drum and Bugle Corps Capital of the World. As a further gesture of their appreciation for Mr. Horlick's generosity toward veterans, state and national branches of the American Legion arranged for five airplanes to fly over the cemetery bowl at the time of services there.

To honor Racine's "first citizen," City Hall, the Racine County Courthouse, and the public schools were closed on the day of the funeral. The local radio station, WRJN, which had frequently received calls from Mr. Horlick requesting that favorite tunes of his be played or sung by staff artists, devoted a special half-hour program of organ music to the memory of William Horlick. It was performed by Ray Gruis. Likewise the "Lum and Abner Pine Ridge" radio program that he had sponsored presented a 15-minute organ concert composed of Mr. Horlick's favorite English folk songs.

Until such time as work on a family mausoleum could be completed, the remains of William Horlick rested in a cemetery vault. The Horlick mausoleum was a commission of the Harrison Granite Company of Chicago and New York. Its grey exterior was simply adorned with symbols of the Episcopal Church. Bronze doors were complemented on either side by bronze-lidded urns. The interior of the mausoleum included a walnut bench, an oriental rug, and a bronze bust of Mr. Horlick. Above the shelf on which the bust rested was a stained glass window depicting a pastoral scene, most likely of his beloved boyhood home in Ruardean. Mr. Horlick's funeral had cost approximately $3,600, the mausoleum, over $36,000.

The Horlick Mausoleum—Mound Cemetery—Racine, Wisconsin
taken by the author

At the time when they commissioned the mausoleum, the remaining Horlick family members likely could not have imagined the short order in which so many of their own deaths would occur. By the time that final work on the structure had been completed in 1938, both Arabella Horlick and Mabelle (Horlick) Sidley had died. Their deaths were followed by that of William Horlick, Jr. just two years later in 1940. At some point, the remains of Alice Priscilla Horlick were moved from their original burial site to the Horlick mausoleum, and following their deaths not even a year apart in 1949 and 1950, A.J. Horlick, and A.J.'s wife, Bertha (Hueffner) Horlick, would also be entombed there. In August of 1963 Mabelle's only child, William Horlick Sidley, long plagued by scandals of his own, died at the age of 50. Survived by his estranged wife, June (Anderson) Sidley and an adopted daughter, Maureen Horlick Sidley, William Horlick Sidley became the last of the family to be entombed in the Horlick mausoleum, following services held for him at the Mound Cemetery Chapel nearby.

In April of 1939, members of the English branch of the Horlick family paid their respects during a visit to the mausoleum at Mound Cemetery, as did Admiral Byrd, who is shown standing alongside William Horlick, Jr. in a photograph taken in front of the mausoleum the year before William Horlick, Jr. died.

When asked how William Horlick would be remembered, a fellow Racinian said this of him:

He was a charming gentleman of the old school....interested in the beautiful and aesthetic things of life...

Frank Starbuck, editor of *The Racine Journal Times* in which the Horlicks held a business interest, had this to say:

I could not help but marvel at his ability to retain so much of what was transpiring, not only in his own business, but all over the world...

H.F. Johnson of S.C. Johnson and Company observed much the same, noting:

I marveled then, as I do now, at the mind of the man. He could joke, run the Boy Scout meeting and tend to his business all at the same time....

One of William Horlick's attorneys remarked that the story of his life, if put in written form, would read like a romance and constitute an inspiration and a sign of hope to every aspiring young man. Judge E.R. Burgess used the words "forward looking" and "progressive" to describe Horlick's accomplishments. Said Burgess:

He made possible to the world a scientific understanding of portions of the earth hitherto unknown. He was not satisfied with aiding and assisting those of the present generation but looking forward into the future, he saw the great opportunity of influencing for good the generations yet unborn by most generously supporting all character-building organizations.

Indeed, groups such as the Boy Scouts and the YMCA could always count on William Horlick when in need. During the time that the YMCA was being built on Wisconsin Avenue in Racine, a question arose over the mortgage. Dr. John G. Meachem, who had been away on a trip, was called back to town and told that $25,000 was needed to settle the issue. "Not knowing what else to do," recalled Meachem, "I went to Mr. Horlick." Without hesitation he wrote out a check for the amount and asked as he handed it to me, "Will that clean up the problem?" "I never told anyone until now because he wouldn't have wanted me to," continued Dr. Meachem, "but now that he's gone, I think people should know. Even his closest associates are unaware of the numerous acts that have benefited mankind."

As word of William Horlick's death reached beyond Racine, thousands of tributes from all over the world began pouring in. Even the luxury ocean liners that he had loved to travel aboard carried the news in their daily papers. But of all the expressions of condolence and recognition brought forth by his dying, the one that William Horlick might have most appreciated was one that echoed a long ago boyhood gesture of his own. While still a young man in Ruardean, he had carved the initials W.H. somewhere on the walls of the village granary. Years later, as they gazed out the windows of the Horlick's Malted Milk factory in Racine, workers would make notations in pencil on the building's wooden pillars—of record snowfalls, the arrival of spring, or the hatching of swans' eggs. A final entry was made on September 25, 1936. It read simply:

Mr. Horlick died at 9:15 a.m. today.

Epilogue—LESSONS LEARNED

When I began this project, my goal was simply to write a brief history of the Horlicks of Racine for a cemetery walking tour guide. Mound Cemetery, where the William Horlick mausoleum is located, dates back over 2,000 years to a time when Native Americans chose to honor their dead by building mounds over their gravesites. It is a cemetery rich in history, with names of local industrialists who founded companies that would one day be internationally known, such as J.I. Case and S.C. Johnson.

Much has been written about the founding and development of those industries, but to my surprise, very little about the Horlicks. And yet here was the story of two creative and inventive brothers, James and William Horlick, who likely gave to the world the beginnings of processed food. Why hadn't more been written about them? Certainly there were scattered pieces to be had, but nowhere, it seemed, a more complete and detailed outline of the Horlick saga. And so it was that I determined to remedy that oversight.

Over the course of several years, I did research in both the Horlicks' native England, in Scotland, and here in Wisconsin where the first Horlick factory was located. Slowly an image of those early years in Ruardean began to emerge, an image of two brothers who were privileged by the standards of their peers, but neither flaunted nor took for granted their good fortunes, as evidenced by their commitment to public service, their dedication to philanthropic endeavors, and their love for the Forest of Dean and those who remained there.

In the realm of thantatalogy (the study of death and dying) there is a concept known as "death guilt," the emotional need on the part of the living to justify his or her life for the sake of those who did not survive. Surrounded as they were at an early age by the gravesites of brothers and sisters who had succumbed to childhood maladies of that time, one wonders what, if any, impact was felt by James and William Horlick and what influence their sense of survivorship may have had on future endeavors.

As fathers, each of them would experience the death of a child. As brothers in business together, they would certainly engage in disagreements, disputes, and outright quarrels. And as with all families, personal relationships and interactions would not always be idyllic. James and William Horlick were, after all, only human.

But that aside, it was what the brothers shared in that was most remarkable. Yes, they made a fortune at it, but together they created a product that sustained and nutured millions of lives. Certainly they and their progeny benefited from the bounteous opportunities that great wealth brings. But think of the steady incomes and attendant opportunities provided to those whom the Horlicks employed worldwide. Churches, schools, hospitals, cultural and recreational facilities as well as innumerable charities were endowed on both sides of "the pond." Developments in human exploration, agriculture, animal husbandry, pharmacy, botanical sciences, education, infant and child care, medicine, and history came about as a result of their support.

There is no question that great wealth carries with it a burden. I personally find it remarkable how well the Horlick family stood up to that challenge. Whatever secrets lie buried with them and, as with each of us, there are some, the fact that two brothers from a tiny village in the Cotswolds would go on to create a personal history that became intertwined with global exploration, two world wars, and most importantly the lives and well-being of millions of people, young and old, whose very existence in many cases depended upon their formula, is testimony enough to their genius as well as to the character of James and William Horlick.

I would like to close the story of James and William Horlick and their legacy with this thought.

It may not be possible to become immersed in a project such as this without coming to feel that, due to proximity, resources, or just plain circumstances, you know one of the individuals better than the others. For me, that one individual would be William Horlick. His adopted hometown of Racine, Wisconsin, was recently characterized in a *New*

York Times article as follows, "Gritty City on the verge of becoming a Hamptons West." Having lived in that "gritty city," for over 30 years, I've often wondered what Racine was really like when William Horlick travelled its streets.

As is true of most American urban areas, little remains that an occupant of nearly 100 years ago might recognize. The original frame factory building, the Horlick home, and that of Mabelle (Horlick) Sidley, known as The Oaks, have all fallen victim to the wrecking ball. William Horlick's favorite local restaurant, Little Bohemia, which remained as a restaurant under a different name, was destroyed by fire. The castle-like structures where Horlick's Malted Milk was produced still stand, but the imposing ivy-covered entry way, flanked by giant evergreens, the elegant swan pond and formal gardens have all disappeared, leaving in their absence shabby old brick buildings in need of tending.

William Horlick High School, sitting on an eleven-acre campus donated by its namesake, only vaguely resembles the architecturally significant edifice it originally was. Missing are the finials, urns and other decorative exterior ornamentations. Inside the school, an extensive collection of artwork given by Horlick's daughter, Mabelle (Horlick) Sidley in her will, is "missing" as well. Even the lovingly prepared and carefully documented photo album put together by Horlick's personal secretary, Andrea Pultz, has somehow "vanished" from the Racine Public Library archives. So too have the bronze coverings on the Horlick mausoleum urns.

This is not to say that nothing of the Horlick legacy remains. St. Luke's Episcopal Church, where the Horlick family worshipped and from where they were buried, looks much as it did when they knew it. The parish house and dining room given by Mr. Horlick are still in use. Extensive redecorating provided for the church sanctuary by Mrs. A.J. Horlick is still in evidence as well. It was in that sanctuary in 1928 that the Reverend Harwood Sturtevant who would later conduct William Horlick's funeral services, read a letter from Mr. and Mrs. Horlick announcing their gift of $125,000 to create the Alice Horlick Maternity Wing at St. Luke's Hospital. Further south on Main Street, at the corner

101

of 10th, one still finds A.J. and Bertha (Hueffner) Horlick's old house, somewhat similar in appearance to that of A.J.'s parents' home. Donated to St. Luke's Hospital as a residence for student nurses, it has since returned to private hands. A few blocks away the elegant cream brick Italianate house where Bertha (Hueffner) Horlick grew up at 1526 College Avenue can be found.

It is worth noting that in death as in life, the remains of two of Racine's world-renowned industrial scions, H.F. Johnson and William Horlick, rest not far from one another in a city-owned cemetery. Fittingly, Horlick Drive wends its richly landscaped way not far from that cemetery. And just down the hill lies the Washington Park High School campus which H.F. Johnson and William Horlick together helped to create.

It was believed by the ancient Greeks that cemeteries were places of learning, schools if you will. Their word for that concept was paiedia. Children who spent time reflecting at the gravesites of their elders would gain insight into history, nature, and the verities surrounding both life and death. I don't remember when I first visited Mound Cemetery, but I do remember being struck by an elaborate arrangement of fresh flowers attached to the bronze doors of the Horlick mausoleum. When later accompanying my Death and Dying students on walking tours of the cemetery, as I often did, I noticed that, regardless of the season, fresh flowers continued to appear at the Horlick mausoleum. Who sent them, I wondered? They were not, as I was aware from serving as a cemetery commissioner, part of the perpetual care program. According to the cemetery office, no one was to know who sent the flowers. For my part, what mattered most was not so much who sent them, but that someone still remembered—whomever that might be.

In the poem by Percy Bysshe Shelley entitled "Ozymandias," we are reminded that no matter how great or far-reaching and remarkable one's deeds or accomplishments, in the end, among the ruins, "nothing beside remains." And while it is true that few tangible reminders of William Horlick's legacy remain, what of the man himself?

Do students and staff who pass through the corridors of Horlick

High School know or care about his devotion to youth and the hopes he had for their future? While being entertained at sporting or musical events, does anyone in the crowd ever wonder how or why Racine came to have Horlick Athletic Field? And on a beautiful spring or autumn day, do strollers through Island/Horlick Park or along Horlick Drive find inspiration, not only in the aesthetics which are so apparent but from the example of one whose generosity made them available for all to share in?

Like the society in which he came to live, William Horlick believed in looking forward and to the future. But he also understood that it is the past which provides us with gratitude and perspective. The way in which he chose to spend his time exemplifies both viewpoints.

Several summers ago a troop of Boy Scouts came to Mound Cemetery looking for a merit badge project. It was suggested that they might uncover and reset the flagstone path leading up to the Horlick mausoleum, which they did. Whatever lessons they learned in the process of restoring that graceful walkway, one thing is for certain, William Horlick would have both appreciated and approved of their efforts.

Gratitude is too often a missing element in our lives. It's hard to be grateful if we don't understand to whom we owe that gratitude. Having "known" James and William Horlick only through what I have heard, read and imagined, I nonetheless remain certain that they are deserving of our gratitude. Over the past months and years they have been, as Carl Sandburg said of Abraham Lincoln, "such good company, not to be forgotten."

Margo Drummond

ABOUT THE AUTHOR

Margo Drummond's interest in local history began when she became involved in Preservation Racine, an organization dedicated to preserving and maintaining community architectural treasures. For that group she wrote a walking tour guidebook for historic Mound Cemetery, which included information on the Horlick mausoleum. The Horlick story piqued her imagination and set her on a quest to learn more. Research was carried out, not only in Racine, but in England and Scotland as well. This book is the result of that research. For 31 years Margo Drummond taught high school courses which included Racine History and Death and Dying, Issues of Living, and Life. She is the author of another book, *Blessings of Being Mortal: How a Mature Understanding of Death Can Free Us to Live Wisely and Well*. Margo lives with her husband Jim in Racine, Wisconsin.

Horlick Advertisement
courtesy Sir John Horlick

Disclaimer

There is a saying that all politics are local. The same may be said of history. When attempting to provide factual information for a project such as this, there are understandably conflicting dates, spellings, and "stories." I have attempted to deal with such conflicting information in as neutral and even-handed a way as possible. A positive outcome of this publication will no doubt be the resolution of disparate observations along with new and previously undisclosed revelations regarding the Horlick legacy.